Gomorrah

To Des

Gomorrah

by

Susan Knight

Illustrations by Marta Wakula

First published in Ireland by Fairground Press 2007

A CIP catalogue record for this book is available from the British Library.

ISBN 978-0-9556349-0-1
Typeset in Book Antiqua 10/16 and Zapfino
Printed and bound by Betaprint, Dublin
Design and Layout by Paula Nolan, Rising Design, Dublin

Fairground Press, 50 Croydon Green, Marino, Dublin 3, Ireland
www.fairgroundpress.com

The Tourist

The city square trembled with light. The sun, catching on the jets of water from the fountains, reflected flickeringly on the faces of passers-by; the sun, shining through shuddering leaves threw flickering shadows. On the shiny bald head of the man sitting at a table of an open-air bar, the man on holiday — or had he really broken all the bonds, had he really left for good? — the man who was observing the scene with pleasure uncomplicated for once by any guilty sense of a duty not fulfilled. He was drinking a refreshing local speciality, a mixture of wine and pomegranate juice, blood-red but ice-cold.

People were milling about. Milling was the word, the tourist thought, because they came and went nowhere but circled the square endlessly, like the numerous pigeons that dodged their feet. There were lovers: the girl in a sleeveless red and orange dress, the man in an open-necked turquoise shirt, embracing constantly and unselfconsciously. At home, the tourist would have disapproved. He would have been embarrassed. But no such stringencies applied here. He smiled indulgently. Such youthful abandon! Such unbridled happiness! The intertwined couple paused in front of some street acrobats, a troupe of midgets and dwarves, bumping and bouncing and falling hilariously. A nun approached the tourist, collecting for some mission, and although he usually didn't, he gave generously because the day was so beautiful and he felt so happy.

A mother wheeled her pram past the bar. The tourist had noticed her before, too. She must have circled the square at least six times. Maybe, if she stopped, the baby would start to cry. Once more she passed the tourist, looking neither to left nor right, past the bar, past the acrobats, past the fountains, under the trees, dappled by sunlight, past the police station inconspicuous but for a fat officer standing on its steps. The tourist was reassured by the presence of the fat officer. It was good to feel that even in strange and exciting foreign cities the rule of law was still upheld. The fat officer stood watching the scene, unconsciously banging the baton held in his right hand off his left.

Across the square, as far as possible from the police station but equally visible to the tourist from his convenient vantage point, groups of traders had their stalls: a peddler selling toys, carved wooden animals, shadow puppets, brightly painted whistles in the form of birds, brightly dressed rag dolls; a fruit seller his cart piled high with polished apples red and green, grapes purple and green, oranges, lemons, grapefruits, aubergines, sweet peppers green, yellow and red, peaches, apricots, cherries, bananas. At another stall a young woman in the uniform of a maidservant was buying armfuls of flowers in all shades of yellow, red and gold, burying her dark head among them in sensuous delight. No doubt attracted by the possibilities, an amateur artist had set up her easel nearby and was recording the scene with impressionistic blobs of colour. Passers-by paused for a minute to look, quickly losing interest and moving on. In a minute, the tourist thought lazily, I will go over and take a look too, and maybe even offer to buy the picture as a souvenir.

The babble of voices, laughter, a shout, the splashing of the fountains, trills of birdsong and the continuous cooing of the pigeons were suddenly drowned out by loud discords: a young man dressed all in black leather and clutching a ghetto blaster was walking through the square in a diagonal line, as though striking it out. He

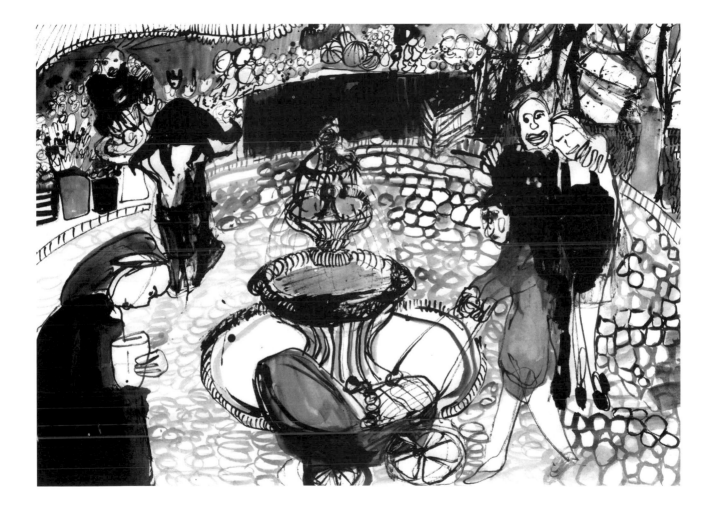

paused, however, to take in a sign advertising a rock concert, the latest sound, a band that even the tourist had heard of, short though his stay in the city had so far been: The Martyrdom of St Sebastian. Goths, the tourist thought distastefully, having hoped to see no more of them.

As he continued to watch, the young man removed from a bag slung over his shoulder a sticker with the message **TONITE!!!** emblazoned on it. This he slapped across the concert notice. Tonight, the tourist thought indifferently. He could go if he wanted to, out of curiosity, to absorb more local colour. Or he could walk the night streets and do the same for free. It was his business and no one else's. He could even go to bed early, if he wished. He had spent his life going to bed early for one reason of duty or another. Now if he wanted to he could go to bed early simply to please himself. He sipped his blood-red drink.

The music faded as the young man went on his diagonal way and a simple tune took its place, a tune played on a tin whistle. It reminded the tourist of something he could not quite remember and he looked round. At first, he could not identify the source of the sound. Then he spotted a piper in deep shade, leaning against a tree, apparently indifferent to the pennies that came his way, playing his melancholy little tune to the pigeons. The tourist closed his eyes and listened, trying hard to remember. It was almost there. He almost had it.

When he opened his eyes again, the piper was blocked from his view by a protester holding high a placard that read **END CORRUPTION NOW**. The fat police officer had seemed to come to attention, the tourist thought. At least, he was banging his baton off his left hand with a greater urgency, a faster rhythm than before. The tourist sighed with pleasure and curled his toes inside his light shoes. He would never go back. Never.

The Woman

The woman was enjoying herself. It made such a difference to get out of that house hung with spiders' webs, to feel again the warm breeze on her face, lifting her hair. She should have done it long ago. To get out among people enjoying themselves, among living people.

Dazzled by the fruit, she bought a lemon and sniffed its pungency. She bought a bag of purple grapes, whose juice seeped through the brown paper so that she had to sit down by the fountain and eat them all at once. Then she rinsed her hands in the flowing water and shook them dry in the sun.

The tourist had noticed her already, but not particularly. She was too dowdy to hold his attention. She reminded him too much of something else, that he didn't want to think about. But whenever he looked at the piper, there she was entranced, listening. When he looked at the acrobats, there she was, laughing her head off. She irritated the tourist slightly, her grey presence in the bright day like a reflection of himself in a mirror of Venetian glass. He watched her approach the peddler selling toys, and buy a rag doll.

"It's for my daughter," he heard her say, unnecessarily. The peddler would only be interested in her money and in the fact that she had not tried to haggle.

"She'll be coming out of school soon. I'm meeting her here."

The peddler counted the coins twice in the hope that she had given him too much.

A burst of children's voices made the tourist turn. Young girls in gym slips poured into the square, many of them greeted by parents waiting there. A large white limousine purred to a standstill right by the bar. A big man in a dazzlingly white suit and white homburg emerged from the limousine and leaned on it, waiting. too. He wore dark glasses, the reflecting kind. He lit up a large cigar. At last it seemed that all of the girls had come out of the school, and those who did not spot their parents at once stood in a giggling group. The big man beckoned over one of these. She skipped up to him and from his side pocket he drew out a bag of bonbons, which he offered to her. She took one and popped it in her mouth while the big man patted her on the head. Then he bent and whispered in her ear, making her giggle again. He opened the car door for her and she hopped in. The big man climbed in beside her and the chauffeur drove off.

Such a pretty scene! At that moment the tourist felt he would have liked a daughter of his own to meet from school, to cosset and spoil. Then he caught sight of the grey woman, still clutching the rag doll, her wild eyes following the car out of the square.

"Buy a flower, buy a lovely flower, one a penny, one little penny..."

A gypsy woman had materialised, flame skirted, her shiny black hair pulled back behind ears from which dangled large gold hoops. A lacy black shawl hung over her bare shoulders. She swayed as she walked, carrying her basket of red carnations. The woman paid no attention as the gypsy brushed by her, continuing her chant.

The lover brought a flower for his mistress, a protester bought one and stuck it on his

placard, the gypsy woman gave another to the fat police officer for free and he stuck it in his lapel.

"Buy a flower, buy a lovely flower for luck, one a penny, one little penny..."

The tourist refused. He had no one to buy a flower for. And he had no need of luck. Not now. He had made his own.

"Everyone needs luck, mister!" The gypsy laughed, a loud cackle, and flashed gold teeth. There was a matching glint in her dark eyes.

"It was you...you I saw," The grey woman had turned and was staring crazily at the gypsy. "It was you."

The gypsy, alarmed now, started to back off. "Not me, lady, not me."

"It was you. What have you done with her?"

"I swear I never done it. I swear it on my mother's soul. Let God be my judge."

The woman, nearly frantic, bore down on the gypsy. Heads turned and an interested crowd started to gather.

"Don't you come near me," the gypsy screeched, and as the woman still tried to grab her, struck out with the bunch of flowers. The red heads flew everywhere.

"It wasn't me. Get away." And a curse in a Romany language.

"It was you," the woman repeated and told the crowd. "I saw her. I saw her clearly."

"What did she do?" people were asking. "Did she rob you?.... A bad lot....Ought to be put away, the whole crew of them... Ought to be shot... Dirty gypsies."

The fat police officer, stirred at last, began to descend the steps ponderously, still banging his baton off his hand.

"I saw her. In my dream. She was in my dream."

"What?.. What did she say?.. In a dream?.. She saw her in a dream?.."

People laughing drew away, tapping their foreheads significantly. The officer relaxed, smelt his flower and again ascended the steps. Only the tourist sat frowning, as if trying to work something out.

The woman stood facing him, her back to the sun-dappled square, her face expressing despair. She was staring fixedly beyond the tourist, who at last turned to see what warranted such attention. He could find nothing.

Suddenly he felt a chill and noticed that a dark shadow had fallen across the square. More than a shadow, the sun was becoming obliterated. Now the crowd stood motionless, looking up. There was a deep stillness. Even the pigeons had stopped cooing, even the fountains were silent. The leaves on the trees shivered once. The wind held its breath.

The tourist frowned again. This was more than a mere cloud covering the sun. But surely there was no eclipse due. It would have been in the papers, on the radio. People would have known. They would have been prepared. He waited. They all did. All except the woman, who was unaware of what was happening and who was still turned away, they all stood waiting for the sun to re-emerge. But the darkness hung motionless. It was hard to see anything now. Someone screamed and then wails and screams rose in a crescendo, turning into ear-blasting shrieks of panic. People rushed in all directions, tripping over each other. A siren sounded briefly, alarm bells went off and then all was silent again. The tourist groped for his lighter and flicked it on. He saw the woman not ten steps from him. She raised her arms in the air and screamed, "My daughter! My daughter!"

A small shiny thing

That night, that endless night, the tourist, shaken by the experience and tired now of too much novelty, would have left the city after all. He would have caught the first plane back home. No one would even have had time to miss him. He would have embraced again gladly the drab yet cosy familiarity that he had so recently sat despising. He would have gone in all haste but for one thing insignificant in itself. A small shiny thing, a knife with a razor edge. The knife in the tourist's back that kept him in his seat, the knife that caused his blood to gush out and mingle inseparably with his abruptly spilt blood-red drink. The knife reclaimed again by a shadowy figure that crept off into the accommodating darkness, carrying as well the tourist's wallet, passport and gold wedding ring.

Surrogate sun

Later that same endless night, the piper came rushing naked into the square. He had earlier climbed the mountain outside the city as if to find the answer to a question that had suddenly been put. He had sat on the top of the mountain playing softly to himself to help himself think, looking alternately down on the few flickering spots of light that marked the city or, when that sight depressed him, out over the dark plain that seemed to stretch into infinity.

There aren't even any stars, he thought. It's almost as if...

Reaching out his hand he seemed to touch some soft, webby material that hid even the sight of his hand from him. He hastily pulled it back. Almost as if....

But the sound of feet treading up the mountain distracted him. Torchlight eerily illuminated fractured outlines of marchers, hundreds of them, each one apparently carrying a stick. The piper, who knew the mountaintop well, decided for some reason to hide in a cleft of the rock. Maybe he wanted to continue uninterrupted his so far unfruitful musings. Maybe he just mistrusted purposeful crowds with sticks. They passed him by and continued on to a flat area on the side of the mountain above the city.

There he saw them by torchlight begin to build a huge pyre with the sticks they had brought. For an hour

they built it up, longer maybe. Who could tell the time without the sun? The piper was stiff, with a crick in his twisted neck from watching and not moving. They lit the pyre at last.

For a while it did not catch but finally burst into wondrous flames. Everyone cheered. Someone, a young girl, started to dance around the pyre and soon people followed her, making up steps as they went, their bodies twisting into strange shapes made stranger by the flickering light, casting cavorting shadows on low clouds. Sparks flew into the sky like fireworks. The crowd danced worshipfully around their surrogate sun. But too soon the fire began to die down and the crowd got frenzied at the thought of having to face the dark again. They started ripping at the few blighted trees and bushes that had so far survived on the mountain. They tore off their clothes and flung them on the flames. Evil smells and yellowish smoke rose from the fire. The people who still danced round the pyre were now naked, now turning crazy with the fumes. The piper wanted to cough but dared not. The people were singing. One word over and over. "BURN BURN BURN BURN..." Again the fire showed signs of dying and a new word was caught by the crowd, a new word that made the piper draw back as far as possible into the cleft of the rock. "SACRIFICE, SACRIFICE..." He knew only too well that poets and dreamers, outsiders, are the first to go in such situations. Who needs them?

He had been spotted. A spark from the fire had floated over and lit up his hiding place for a second, illuminating his white face. He was not even recognised, only as an interloper. The crowd rushed towards him. Flesh was needed to propitiate the gods of darkness. Flesh that would burn long and slow, like a tallow candle.

The piper tore off his clothes and threw them to the mob. In the pause that followed, as they picked them up and sniffed them, he took off down the mountainside with an agility he had not known himself to possess. Unlike his pursuers, he knew the way. From living rough for so long his skin had hardened and become impervious to the prickles that was tearing their flesh open, causing their blood to drip on the rocks, on the heather. He lost his pursuers but stopped only when he burst like a tornado into the square, only then conscious of his nakedness.

A sliver of moonlight

The singer was no stranger to darkness. She was at home in it, it was her milieu. She stood fearlessly at the doorway of the bar looking out at the empty square, wondering where everyone had gone. She did not notice the huddled and trembling clusters of people just outside the pools of dim illumination cast by the few street lamps, bulbs caught in among the leaves of trees so that even at night the light flickered. She saw only the lone man at the table and nearly went over to him. Then she remembered hazily that he was the dead tourist with the knife wound in his back and wasn't it about time someone took him away? No wonder business was slack. She started to sing softly to herself. Then something caught her attention and she lifted heavy eyes up towards the sky. There was a fire on the mountain but she had no idea what it might mean. A fire on the mountain? The mountain was not, as far as she knew, a volcano. While she watched she saw what looked like a sliver of moonlight streak down the mountainside. But there was no moon. Suddenly the naked piper fell into the square, almost at her feet, his body streaked and beaded. She stared puzzled at him for a while. Then she pulled a tablecloth off one of the tables and crossed slowly to the fountain where she soaked the cloth in water. Slowly, slowly, she crossed back to the naked man and wiped him with it. He shuddered at her touch and at the icy coldness of the water. Slowly, slowly she crossed to the table of the dead tourist. She pulled the light linen jacket off his body and laid it on the ground. Then she loosened his new linen trousers, hardly spattered with blood at all, and pulled them off too. The dead tourist had thin grey legs with hairs all over them. He wore green socks with clocks. She slowly carried the trousers and jacket over to the naked piper, flickering silver in the light from a street lamp. He put on the clothes, apparently not noticing the bloodstained gash in the back of the jacket, nor the spatters of blood and wine on the new trousers. The piper was still holding his tin whistle. He started to play a tune that the singer seemed to remember from somewhere. She watched him as he walked away from her, still playing, his silver skin visible through the gash in the back of the jacket.

The face in the mirror

The woman had been searching for hours. She had searched the same places over and over again; she had searched in places where she knew to search was hopeless. She had asked and asked and asked and people had looked at her with blank faces. Why should they care about her loss? Didn't they have losses of their own?

She had returned reluctantly to the webby house and had peered into every corner. Even into the dark mirror where for once she saw only herself. Disturbed spiders scurried off. Maybe her daughter had fallen

asleep in the middle of a game as children do, but the house echoed emptily to her cries. She still clutched the rag doll to herself. It provided a kind of comfort.

The woman circled her way back to the city square. Wasn't it there that she had caught a glimpse? If only it wasn't so dark. If only she could remember properly. She poked at huddled groups of people. Little girls turned wan faces up to her. But not the one she wanted.

In the square, she accosted at last a man with a familiar face in unfamiliar clothes — could that really be blood on the torn back?

"Your daughter? How should I know if I've seen your daughter?"

The familiar rebuff. She turned away.

"Wait!" he called. She had been right. He was kinder than the others.

"I've searched everywhere," she said.

"Impossible. Anyway, while you were searching over here, she might have been over there, searching for you. And when you were over there, maybe she came over here. You see that, don't you."

She supposed that she did.

"But I've searched everywhere."

"What does she look like, your daughter?"

The woman thought. She tried to see the face in the dark mirror.

"Well, it's hard to say really. A child."

"Is she dark?"

"No."

"Fair, then."

"Well..."

"Or red haired with light skin?"

"Er..."

"And green eyes... and freckles?"

"You've seen her!"

The woman saw now, in the mirror, smiling.

"No," the piper admitted. "Well, I don't know, of course. I might have. But at the time I didn't know it was her, if you understand me."

He looked at the woman's puzzled, troubled face and wished he could play what he meant on his pipe. But meaning clotted on his tongue.

"No," the woman said, "I don't understand anything."

"If you like," he said, because he was indeed sometimes kind and because he had nothing else to do and nowhere to go, "we can look for her together."

Across the square, the singer in the doorway of the bar saw the woman seize the piper's hand with joy and dance off with him. The singer turned back into the bar just as a mother pushing a pram circled the square, slowly and steadily.

Later on, when the square was quiet again, when the fire on the mountain glowed with a dull light that illuminated nothing, some shadows grouped around the body of the dead tourist still slumped at the bar table. When they had finished, the dead tourist sprawled naked, face down on the ground, even his false teeth taken from him, even his new green socks with clocks.

The authorities are our only hope

The queue stretched across the square, weaving between the trees, circling the fountain. It did not have the fellowship of most queues. The people shuffled forward, up the steps of the police station, heads bent, silent. The woman was standing arguing with the piper. She wanted to go in. He was trying to discourage her.

They had searched for hours, covering ground already covered, asking people already asked.

"The authorities are our only hope," the woman was saying.

"I shouldn't bother with them, if I were you."

"They're here to serve the community."

The piper smiled sardonically. "To serve the community! Is that what it's called?"

"They're our only hope," the woman repeated. "There's no harm in trying."

"Are you sure?"

"What's wrong? Do you have a record or something?"

"A golden disc, actually." The piper smiled again. "You don't mind if I wait outside. These places usually bring me out in cuts and bruises."

"The innocent," the woman stated sanctimoniously, "have nothing to fear."

She shuffled forward with the others, leaving the piper under a tree. He leaned against it and took his tin whistle from the pocket of the bloodstained jacket. Again he started to play one of those sad little songs that sounded so unaccountably familiar to those who heard them. Again the singer came to the door of the bar. She gazed at the piper with her smoky eyes but never once did he look back at her.

Later, as the woman was shuffling up the steps of the police station, head bent, like the rest of the petitioners — but not cowed like them, only absorbed in her problems — a sudden noise made her turn. A procession of protesters were marching into the square carrying placards, and as they marched, they chanted the message on the placards:

END POLICE BRUTALITY
CIVIL RIGHTS FOR POLITICAL PRISONERS
STOP CORRUPTION NOW
NO TORTURE OF DETAINEES

In the police station, officers paused in their work to listen. One, writing a report, snapped his pen in half. Another scratched his damp armpit thoughtfully. Another, interrogating a suspect, turned the screw just that fraction tighter, smiling grimly. The suspect told him something interesting, then fainted away.

Down below the police station, in subterranean cells, prisoners of crime and of conscience sat on the edges of their cots or stood, if they were still able to, and banged on their walls chanting **"FREEDOM, FREEDOM"**. Although by then few, if any, knew what the word meant.

The woman shuffled steadily up the last flight of stairs. She could now see the desk of the officer on duty. He was processing claims at a break-neck speed. Outside, the woman could hear the chant of the protesters. It seemed to do nothing for the good temper of the officer on duty. He was fat, and sweat, under the unshaded light bulb, dripped off him.

"Next!" he called.

The woman shuffled forwards.

"It's my daughter," she said.

"What?" The officer wrote something on a form.

"I can't find her."

"Who?"

"My daughter. I've looked everywhere."

"It's very common. Happens all the time these days. A little tot gets lost in the dark."

The woman was grateful for his kind understanding. The piper had, of course, been wrong.

"She'll turn up." The officer was decisive, dismissive.

"Can't you do anything?"

The officer sighed. This was the sixty-ninth case of a missing person he had dealt with in the past two hours. Didn't these people know anything?

"We'll alert all duty officers of course, Mrs er Watt."

He looked at her for the first time. A worn, grey, dowdy woman, as he might have expected. The sort any husband would run a mile from. Any man. Unless it were dark. They were all the same in the dark. And of course it was dark now. Very dark. Unprecedentedly dark. He smiled at her. Take her clothes off and she would do, he thought. In the dark.

"Now, if you could just give me a description of the little girl."

"Well..."

"Fair?"

"No..."

The officer wrote "dark".

"Age?"

The woman started to sob. "She's very small."

"Now, now," the officer was starting to get bored.

"What was she wearing?"

"Wearing?"

"Was she coming from school?"

The woman stared at his prescience, then nodded.

"Uniform, then." he wrote the word. "Stop crying please," peremptorily. "This is a public place. I tell you she'll turn up. Next."

F|2143360

The woman tried to protest but she couldn't control her crying. An old man behind her nudged her smartly out of the way. As she turned to go, the officer eyed her hunched back with distaste. He couldn't stand weepers. Reminded him of his smother. Mother, he meant. No (laughing at his own joke) smother was it all right. He screwed up the form and tossed it in the bin. The old man was complaining of a dead body in the square. The officer sighed. Another one.

The woman dropped on to the stairs for a moment. She was utterly exhausted. She had been searching for hours. She had been standing in line for hours. She had forgotten to eat or drink. Now she succumbed.

A foot caught her in the back. The booted foot of an officer.

"No cluttering up the stairs."

The woman nearly toppled forward. She was caught in time by an old crone.

"You look all in," the crone whispered.

At that moment, the door of the Police Commissioner's office opened. The Commissioner himself, his half-hundredweight of meat held together by his trim bemedalled uniform, stepped out, his great arm around the shoulders of another big man, in a white suit, white homburg and reflecting sunglasses.

The Commissioner was smiling fatly.

"Rest assured, my dear sir," he was saying, "that matter will be attended to immediately. It will be the subject of our undivided attention."

The two men walked side by side down the stairs where so recently the woman had slumped. Now she drew in with the rest against the wall. The Police Commissioner clicked his fingers. An officer ran up. The

Commissioner whispered instructions into the officer's ear. The officer saluted and ran out.

"That's how it is done here, my dear sir," the Commissioner informed the man in white. "We spare no effort, waste no time in the pursuit of our duties and the protection of our citizens."

Although her shoulder hurt from the kick from the officer's boot, it warmed the woman to hear such reassuring words. Surely with such an attitude to the job, they would soon find her daughter. Unlike the others in the queue who kept their heads bent, she gazed with frank admiration at the Commissioner. A fine man, if somewhat overweight. She was amazed then at the size of the wad of notes that passed from the podgy paw of the man in

white to the equally podgy paw of the Commissioner. He caught her eye and looked displeased.

"A contribution," he said fruitily, as he pocketed the wad, "to the widows and orphans of officers' fund is always appreciated, my dear sir."

The man in white managed to laugh heartily without emitting a single sound. He left the building, escorted by several men in black leather, while the Commissioner started back up the stairs to his office.

The woman turned to the old crone who had been kind to her.

"Who was the man in white?" she asked. "He looked familiar to me."

The old crone had no teeth to speak of. She whispered unintelligibly.

"What did you say?"

"Mr El Blanco. Shh..." The crone whispered louder.

The Police Commissioner turned and looked right at her. The old crone gasped and held her hand to her toothless mouth. Then she hobbled out as fast as she could. More slowly, the woman descended the stairs. The name meant nothing to her.

Outside, the protesters continued to chant. A white limousine was being driven slowly across the square. The piper stood under his tree. The singer stood in the bar doorway staring at him with her smoky eyes. The dead tourist's naked body lay sprawled on the ground. The white limousine stopped in front of the bar, a door opened and a hand beckoned. The singer stepped over the dead tourist and got in. The limousine drove away. Up on the mountain, the fire died into a dull glow.

The woman crossed to where the piper stood.

"Any joy?" he asked.

"They said they would alert all officers."

The piper laughed.

"Why are you so cynical?" the woman asked.

The piper shrugged. He knew that for the time being the woman wanted to believe and knew that nothing he could say would shake her.

"Tell me something," the woman went on. "Who is Mr El Blanco and why is everyone so afraid of him?"

The piper looked at her

"You really don't know anything, do you," he said softly.

"Tell me, then," she persisted. She knew that in the webby house she had forgotten a great many things.

The piper told her that Mr El Blanco was the boss of bosses. "The big boss. *Comprende*?"

"I remember now where I saw him before." The woman looked in the mirror. Sometimes it cleared. "It was in the square before... before it went dark. He was collecting his daughter from school, just like anyone else."

The piper paused. She really knew nothing.

"His daughter?"

The woman explained how it was. "He called her over and even had sweets for her. I wished I had bought sweets for my daughter. So you see, he can't be all bad."

"He has no daughter," the piper said.

"A friend's daughter then."

"He has no friends. His friends have no daughters."

The woman understood nothing. "Then who?"

"Maybe," the piper said slowly, "it was your daughter."

The woman looked at him.

"Oh no," she said, remembering now what she had thought at the time, "it couldn't have been." That damned mirror.

"Perhaps we should go and see," the piper said to her, very softly.

"Where can we go? What can we see?" she asked puzzled. Hadn't they already been everywhere?

"We've only searched a fraction of the possible places," the piper said. "Perhaps we haven't even searched the most likely places. I didn't want to take you there. But after what you've told me..."

"What are you talking about? Where haven't we been?"

"To the Street of Innocents," the piper said.

The innocent have nothing to fear

Some time after the piper and the woman had left the square, the Commissioner, who had been sitting in his office stroking his smooth and silky chin and nibbling prawn crackers, perked up his ears and muttered to himself. "At last."

Beyond the monotonous chant of the protesters — they could really keep that sort of thing up for hours — and the rattles and bangs from the dungeons — half rations at supper for them again — he heard the sound he had been waiting for. He pulled his pork out of the swivel chair it was wedged in, and crossed the soft carpet, so thick and soft his footprints showed in it for a few seconds until the crushed pile sprang back. He opened his heavy door and faced again the miserable rabble on the stairs. Petitioners, complainants, informers — no, informers went round the back and didn't have to wait, how could he forget. He pushed down the stairs, enjoying the way the crowd, eyes downcast, drew back from him. He pushed out of the door, holding his baton. He stood for a while, legs apart, banging, as if unconsciously, his baton off his meaty left hand, watching the protesters.

"Move along there," he said at last.

The protesters ignored him, or rather, started to chant even louder.

"Move along there," he said again, mildly, smiling.

"We're not doing any harm," a protester told him.

"You're causing an obstruction." Still smiling.

"Not at all." The protester's sparsely bearded face was haloed in long curly hair. He looked like Christ. A hippie! The Commissioner spat, neatly spraying the protester's sandalled foot. Wiping it with a raggedy handkerchief, the protester continued calmly, "We're taking care to keep out of people's way."

"And," the Commissioner continued as if he hadn't heard a word, "you're liable to cause a breach of the peace."

"Hardly," the Christ-like protester continued, "That's your privilege, Commissioner."

The Commissioner smiled. He could afford to. He knew something these charlies didn't.

"Move along, sonny, before I lose my temper."

The protesters sat down. The Commissioner closed his eyes in ecstasy.

"Like that, is it? OK, sonny boys and girls..." He blew his whistle. From behind the protesters, blocking their exit in all directions, advanced the hundred-strong back-up team he had called up, street lamps flickering blue-black on their armour. They advanced slowly and steadily, the twenty or so protesters huddling closer. The glittering blue-black squad of riot cops halted. The Commissioner contemplated the scene with satisfaction, then raised his whistle to his lips and blew two short sharp blasts. The riot cops baton-charged the twenty or so protesters while the Commissioner watched in delight as if at the movies. Really, he thought, it was much better than the movies. A full-breasted woman clasping a baby was dragged off to the cells, her skirt up round her waist. He looked at her hairy legs in disgust. Hippies! The Christ-like protester was under six or seven cops. The Commissioner hoped that no one would actually get killed if only for the sake of the additional paper-work, but he would like that Jesus freak to get his come-uppance. He blew his whistle again, once, and jerked his head. The rest of the protesters were dragged off to the cells, along with a few unfortunate petitioners and others who happened to be in the way. The amateur artist for one, still trying to capture the scene on canvas. Her easel and paints were trampled on the ground, her pictures ripped.

Before he returned to his office, the Commissioner looked across the now empty square. Empty but for the body near the bar. That fucking corpse, he thought to himself.

The Street of Innocents

The Street of Innocents was at the other end of town from the square, reached through a maze of dingy lanes lined with run-down houses. There was no sound except for the occasional cat-fight, a yelling baby, a radio with the volume briefly turned up.

The woman could hear the clop clop of her shoes echoing along the pavements. The piper, for his part, walked softly. He had picked up some discarded rubber-soled sandals that fitted him well enough. The woman thought to herself that she would not like to wear some unknown and perhaps dead person's shoes, but the piper didn't seem to mind. As for his ragged and bloodstained jacket, it was better not to think about it at all.

She couldn't remember ever visiting this part of town before. She rather thought she didn't even know of its existence. They had crossed a footbridge over a stinking canal and had seemed thereafter to be in another country.

Smoke came inexplicably out of alleyways, shadowy figures seemed to slip ahead of them, beside them, but just out of focus. Alone, the woman would have been terrified, but the piper seemed confident and unafraid. Surely, the woman thought, my daughter wouldn't have come here.

A red glow hung in the sky in front of them. Not another fire! Bonfires were being lit everywhere. But this glow just hung, unflickering, in the sky. They turned a corner. The woman stopped abruptly: here was hell.

Red lights shone in doorways or recesses. Barely-clad men and women stood or reclined languidly. Other men stood alertly. Yet more men, men in suits, walked up and down, eyeing everyone else. Everyone seemed to be smoking. Clouds of pink smoke rose into the air.

The woman turned to the piper.

"Where have you brought me? There are no children here. This is no place for children."

"Do you have money?" the piper asked her.

"What?"

"Give it to me."

The woman rummaged in her pockets.

"I hope I can trust you," she said. She gave the piper two notes.

"You can," he assured her, "with your life."

He told her to wait as he approached a man in a shiny open-necked turquoise shirt and green silk trousers. With his sleek blond hair and sharp features the man looked like some sort of reptile or snake. The piper whispered to the man and gave him some money. The man then called over a fat girl in a transparent black nylon blouse over a skimpy bikini. The fat girl took the piper by the hand and he beckoned the woman to follow.

"What is this?" she hissed. "Where are you taking me?"

The fat girl led them into a recess and up a dirty flight of stairs. The dark was thicker here and several times the woman trod on something that squelched under her foot. There was an unpleasant odour which she could not identify. They seemed to be climbing and crossing passages for an extraordinary length of time before stopping before a door. The fat girl jerked her head towards it.

"Give her something," the piper said.

"What?"

"A coin, something, then she'll go away."

The fat girl stood blankly.

The woman took out two coins and pressed them into the fat girl's cold, wet hand. She rolled off.

The piper waited until she was out of sight and then opened the door. In a room furnished only with a rumpled bed and illuminated by red light coming through the window from the street outside, a girl child in school uniform was playing with a rag doll. It was identical in all respects to the rag doll the woman was still holding.

"What is this?" the woman asked in dread.

The piper crossed over to the child, who looked up at him with expressionless eyes, like those of the fat girl. He patted her reassuringly on the head.

"This is the girl who was abducted from the square today by Mr El Blanco. The pimp downstairs told me she was a virgin but I guess," pointing to dry blood on the girl's leg, "that she has already been violated many times."

"What are you saying!" The woman rushed to the child and embraced her. "She's no more than eight or nine years old."

She suddenly held the child slightly away from her. The child turned blank eyes towards her.

"There's something wrong."

But almost instantly the child looked more alert. A car was being driven slowly up the street. It stopped. Three measured toots sounded from a horn. The child wriggled out of the woman's grasp and raced from the room.

The piper crossed to the window and looked down.

"Come," he said.

The woman joined him. The white limousine was parked in the street, its engine purring like a cat that is being stroked. It was surrounded by children, boys and girls who came rushing from doorways. Behind them the barely-clad men and women waited. The woman observed the fat girl among them.

Mr El Blanco climbed out and waved at them all. He fondled a small boy who grabbed his leg. A man in a black leather suit passed Mr El Blanco a large bag. He started giving out something from the bag to the children. The little girl lately beside them pushed forwards to the front of the group. Mr El Blanco gave her something from the bag, too, and whispered or blew in her ear, making her giggle.

The piper turned to the woman and said softly, "See how Mr El Blanco loves his children. See how kind he is. See how devoted they are to him. He comes regularly to give them bonbons. The bonbons taste good, you see. And they kill the pain. And they help you to forget."

Tears ran down the woman's face. The piper wiped them away tenderly with his fingers.

"So anyway," he went on, "your daughter is not here?"

The woman peered over the windowsill, scanning the faces in the crowd. She shook her head. She looked again for the little girl. Red-haired with freckles and green eyes. The child was sitting on the kerb sucking her bonbon. An old man with spittle falling from his lips, and wearing an evilly stained business suit, passed and repassed. Finally, the old man approached the snake-like pimp in the shiny turquoise shirt and spoke to him. Money changed hands. The old man grabbed the little girl hungrily by the arm and began to walk off with her.

"Can't we do something?" the woman asked the piper.

"Not unless you want your throat slit. Come, let's go."

"And leave her?" the woman asked, agonised.

The piper caressed her face.

"She's just had her bonbon," he said. "She won't feel anything, I promise."

They made their way out along winding corridors and down dark slimy staircases — the piper seemed to know his way. They passed a dark recess. From within, a child screamed and the piper had to use all his strength to drag the woman away.

Where women once

There were bonfires all over the city. A fire had even been lit in the square. The protesters' placards burned steadily and well. The fountains, reflecting back the flickering flames, seemed to be flowing molten gold at first, then as the fire died down, blood. The mother with the pram paced the square. It certainly worked. The baby never let out a single murmur.

Leather and chain-clad rock fans sat on the edge of the fountain, their music blaring, their white faces eerily lit. They drank beer from large plastic bottles. Occasionally they pissed into the fountain, their urine a long golden stream in the firelight. One of them crossed idly to investigate the body of the dead tourist, still lying under a table outside the bar. He kicked it probingly with his high-heeled black boot. Even to him, high and rising fast, it seemed strange that such a thing should be left lying around, even under the present unusual circumstances. You'd have thought someone would cover it up at least, with a tablecloth for instance. There were still several tablecloths on the tables. He would do it himself only the lads might mock. He gave the dead tourist one last prod, lifting the withered grey penis with the toe of his cowboy boot and letting it drop back. He returned to the lads with a coarse remark and they all laughed.

The flames from the last of the placards crackled and sparks flew upwards.

END POLICE BRUTALITY.

Down in the cells, low moans came from protesters still conscious. The full-breasted woman with the small child rocked to and fro, the child dozing and crying in turn on her lap. Was it something to be thankful for that some masked and helmeted police officer, stinking incidentally of pungent sweat, had dragged the two of them from the square before the systematic beatings started? Neither of them had worse injuries than bruises. But the child was hungry and thirsty and the woman had no milk to suckle her. The woman started to sing softly. Not a song of protest but a folk song from the mountains of a wild west country where the ocean was slowly winning its battle against the rocky cliffs, beating them down century by century. Where women once keened for their menfolk, fishermen claimed by the jealous sea. The woman sang softly and, after a while, in the distance, outside the cells, the plaintive sound of a pipe took up her tune.

In another cell the protester to whom the Commissioner had taken a particular dislike tasted blood in his mouth and knew that some of his teeth were broken. His head was throbbing violently and he feared for his ribs because every time he tried to move, pain shot through his chest. He too heard the sad song of loss and longing but couldn't think at all. Nothing linked the broken images in his head. He lost consciousness again and seemed to be floating out to sea on choppy waves that held him up like the hands of mermaids.

Away across the city, the singer stood in a room lined with velvet. She wore nothing but a golden bandage wound around her body many times. She sang the blues in her low throaty voice while Mr El Blanco ate dead skylarks with his fingers, crunching tiny bones in his mouth. Sometimes he took gulps of expensive French wine from a crystal goblet. After a while he washed his hands in a finger bowl on which white rose petals floated. He was a stickler for personal hygiene. He wiped his hands dry on a fluffy warm towel then beckoned the singer over. He caught one end of the golden bandage and started to unravel it. Spinning her round slowly. She closed her eyes and thought of the silver skin of the piper.

Double maxiburger with chips

The Commissioner wiped greasy hands on his trousers, then felt guilty. His wife would give him hell. She was always telling him to mind his trousers. He screwed up the bag that had held the just consumed kebab and flung it in the bin by his desk, missing it. He was in a foul temper. What a day!

Why did people keep expecting him to know what had happened. He wasn't a scientist, was he? How was he supposed to know anything about it? Even his wife had phoned. Where's the sun gone? she had asked. We've put it under arrest, dear. For exposing itself in a public place.

It was those bloody protesters. Like fleas, irritating, biting, preventing him from getting on with the job. He had probably over-reacted. One of the buggers had been rushed to hospital with a brain haemorrhage. His superiors would say he over-reacted. They didn't have to deal with the buggers, day in day out, holier than thou, hairy-legged women, hairy-faced men. We-will-overcome types. Who the fuck did they think they were fooling, anyway. Didn't they know the battle was already lost?

Jesus, he was hungry again. Starving. Well, of course there was nothing in those kebabs. Nothing substantial. The dough was like blotting paper. Then there was El Blanco. The man was getting above himself. The Commissioner patted his pocket. A nice little sum, nonetheless. But when you thought what he had to do for it. The things he was expected to turn a blind eye to. It was beyond a joke. And, by the time everyone had taken a piece, what was left for him was laughable. Not worth risking everything for, anyway. And he was worried. Informers had been bringing worrying news lately. Not about the protesters. They were up front, village idiots. You knew where you stood with them. But the informers were talking about an organisation. The Black Death it called itself, with cells springing up everywhere, dedicated to little more than destruction, but destruction of authority, law and order, power. Destruction probably of the police, first off. Cells everywhere, apparently. And then, to cap it all there was that damned body in the square. He spat, this time accurately on the desk photograph of his dear wife. The gob ran down her many times lifted and ghoulishly simpering face. He summoned an officer and ordered him to fetch a double maxiburger with chips, side portion of coleslaw and whipped shake, strawberry flavour. The prospect already made him feel slightly better.

The woman dragged her feet after the piper along an unfamiliar street. She couldn't believe that, having lived all her life in this city — most of it, admittedly, indoors — there was so much that was unknown to her. She was ready to drop but knew at the same time that she must go on. Still, she dropped. Her legs buckled under her. The piper strode on for a while unnoticing and the woman had not even the energy to call him back.

She rested her aching back against a dank and ripping wall. She peered at the looming buildings all around her. Maybe this place wasn't so strange after all. Maybe it was just the darkness that made it seem so. Maybe round the next corner was the dim house with the spidery corners, the dim corridor with the mirror whose reflection she always seemed just to miss.

Once there had been a conservatory, she remembered, with a glass door leading to a rose garden. The conservatory caught the sun. Huge tomato plants grew there and gave off a choking, tropical smell. The air was heavy. In an instant your clothes were soaked in sweat. You could hardly breathe. Then you opened the door into the rose garden and drank in the cool and aromatic air, the light breezes in the aromatic rose garden seeming like a gentle caress after the conservatory's choking grip.

The piper was stroking her face.

"You came back," she muttered.

"You're all in, poor thing."

She wanted to be back in the rose garden. The drips from the wall had soaked into the back of her dress. Evil smells emitted from steaming drains.

"Come," the piper said, "I'll carry you."

She was a small woman, very light. He strode along the street carrying her, until a flickering sign indicated a café. He put her down and they entered. Shadowy figures crowded round a bar. Mask-faced women flicked soiled boas in their direction. A filthy tramp stank quietly. Some teenagers sat furtively in a corner, their eyes on the shadowy figures. The piper set the woman at a table and went to the bar and ordered tea and rolls. A fat old woman with a crooked ginger wig and orange lipstick on her false teeth brought over the order. She smiled sexily at the piper and pushed her armour-plated bosom towards him. He smiled back at her and gave her a big tip with the woman's money.

The woman could barely get her teeth into the dry roll. Finally, despairingly, she took the piper's example and dipped the roll into her tea. That at least was strong, sweet, hot and reviving. She now realised that she had become light-headed with hunger.

One of the teenagers finally got up and crossed to the shadowy figures at the bar. Money appeared to change hands and the teenager returned to his companions smiling broadly and clasping a small package. They all got up and left. The piper watched them.

"I'd bet at least one of them won't last the night," he said. The endless night.

The woman was too tired to ask what he meant. She put her head on her arms on the table and fell into a dream-filled sleep.

She was trying to get into the rose garden but the conservatory door was locked and she seemed to have lost the key. She searched and searched; the sun blazed down on the conservatory and it grew hotter and hotter. Over-ripe tomatoes fell splat splat splat on the floor around her. The musty smell of the plants overcame her and she too fell to the floor and into a dream-filled sleep.

She was in the spidery house. She was climbing the stairs to her darling's room. It was dark and she kept treading on soft, slidy things. She could see the door of her darling's room up ahead of her but the higher she climbed, the further away it seemed. The door suddenly swung open. The room beyond was brightly, dazzlingly lit. The woman crawled on hands and knees the last few steps to the doorway of the room. Before the door slammed shut in her face she had glimpsed what was beyond. She screamed.

She opened her eyes. She had closed them only for a moment. Everything was the same.

The piper's silver skin shone where the jacket now hung open in front. There was a smear of orange on his ear. The old woman with the crooked wig — even more crooked than before, it seemed — stood laughing silently behind him.

"We must go!" the woman cried out. "I've wasted so much time."

"Go where?" the piper asked. "I've run out of ideas."

"Go to the fairground, love," the old woman said, her false teeth clicking. "It's a great show."

"The fairground!" the woman repeated in disgust. The old woman was truly repellent. "We're not out and about for the purposes of entertainment, you know."

"The fairground," said the piper. "That's not such a bad idea."

The woman looked at him. Of course, he'd had enough of this trailing around. She had always known he would give up.

"I don't know why I didn't think of it before."

"What?"

"Did you never take your daughter to the fairgound? Did she never see the clowns, the acrobats, the novelty acts?"

The woman thought.

"I don't remember. Perhaps. Why?"

"The acrobats were in the square today. Maybe she ran off with them to join the fairground folk."

The woman laughed then, out loud.

"What a ridiculous idea!"

"Think back," the piper persisted. "Did you never want to do it? Were you really never grabbed by the foolish romantic notion to throw it all up and follow a dream. The fairground, the circus. Free as air, soaring above the multitude, leaping among the lions, riding bareback in sequins and gauze."

What a ridiculous person he was after all! The smear of orange on his ear gave him an almost clownish appearance himself.

"Of course not," the woman said with dignity. "I had a very contented childhood." The rose garden. Ah!

"Don't tell me you never had dreams," the fool continued. "All children dream. Some adults, too."

My darling's door. Ah!

"It would never," she stated firmly, "have entered my daughter's head."

"Are you sure you know her well enough to say that. Dreams are very private, you know."

"She's my daughter. I know everything about her."

The mirror, the swaying curtain. Ah!

"Well, that's to say..."

Whose was that stranger's face? She could almost remember.

"But isn't it worth trying? Isn't it? No stone left unturned and all that... Don't turn your nose up like that. Some of my best friends are fairground folk."

The woman assented at last, wearily.

"Oh all right. It can't do any harm to try."

As they rose to leave, the old woman with the crooked wig crossed over to them carrying a loud chocolate-and-banana coloured hound's-tooth checked jacket. She rubbed her armour plated bosom against the piper.

"You can't go around in that," she purred, fingering the dead tourist's sleeve. "Questions will be asked. You could land yourself in deep water, darling. Take this one. It belonged to my last husband. He won't be wanting it again." She wheezed with laughter.

"It's stunning," the piper said. He took off the dead tourist's blood-marked jacket. His hairless body flashed silver, like a streak of moonlight. He tried on the last husband's jacket. It was big and baggy and made him look even more like a clown.

"Thank you," he said to the old woman.

She kissed him on the lips, leaving a trace of orange around his mouth.

"Thank you," he said again.

Sweet cake

Down in the cells, the full-breasted woman rocked her child on her lap. A policeman in a mask and helmet had brought down milk and sweet cake for her and the child, and had stood over them while they ate it in case other prisoners might grab it off her or in case she felt inclined to share. She looked like the kind of woman who would share, he thought. He still remembered how her soft body had felt when he dragged her into the police-station away from the riot. She, of course, didn't know it was him: all policemen in riot gear look the same. She was wary and peeped at him as she fed the child, as if fearing that this was another trick. That she would have to pay for the food with a beating or even with sex. Some pigs were like that. But this one stood apparently staring down at her — his mask anyway had been pointing towards her — still smelling pungently of sweat.

Then he just left, leaving her to rock the child to sleep.

Much later, she along with most of the protesters and those arrested in error were freed, although the so-called ring-leaders, including the protester who reminded the Commissioner of Christ, were detained to be interrogated. The amateur artist was also detained for some reason, although she had been nowhere near the protesters and clearly had nothing to do with them.

The full-breasted woman left the station carrying the still sleeping child. She had no intention of communicating with the others, not here, not under the blue light of the station lamp. She would go home and rest.

She scuttled through the dark streets, unaware of the masked and helmeted figure that followed behind her like a shadow.

A blue and purple flame

In the seedy café, the old woman with the crooked wig called to the old tramp who was slumped in a corner. She helped him peel off the steaming coat he was wearing and put on the dead tourist's linen jacket with the blood-rimmed gash on the back. The old woman threw the tramp's steaming coat out into the street where later it was picked up and burnt on a bonfire, flaming for an instant magnificently blue and purple.

The old tramp displayed his new jacket proudly to the mask-faced women, who flicked their soiled boas at him. The shadowy figures at the bar laughed into their whiskey. Meanwhile, out in the basement of a nearby alleyway, among decaying heaps of rubbish, four teenage boys smoked strangely scented cigarettes until one by one they keeled over and collapsed.

The wedding viel

The Commissioner bit into a tuna salad roll. Thousand islands dressing and tomato pips dripped on to his trousers. His wife would go crazy. He glanced at her photograph: the spittle still hung on it, like a veil over her grimly simpering features. It reminded him of his wedding day. How at last she had lifted the veil and he had seen her for what she was. Troubles, troubles. Later, for dessert, he would go and interrogate the protesters. He smiled greasily at the thought. Now he phoned an officer and ordered an ice-cream soda, cola-flavoured, to wash down the roll.

Easy

The full-breasted woman protester at last reached the vast house where she had a room. The child still slept. The masked and helmeted figure still followed noiselessly. It was as he had thought. She lived alone. There was no husband or lover. The husband or lover would surely have been at her side if he existed. She was no doubt easy with her favours, easy and relaxed. He remembered how her body had felt against him, first trying to be hard, struggling, then, after he had hit her across the face, suddenly quiet, and soft, so soft. He rubbed the hand that had hit her face across his lips. He settled down to wait.

Freaks

By now, they had walked almost out of the city, the piper and the woman. The fairground tents were erected on an old bombed site that served as a park for the inhabitants of the high-rise flats erected to house those driven out by inner-city slum clearance.

The flats stood now monolithic in the dark, dim lights visible from a few windows, like sinister misplaced eyes.

Across the city, the bonfire on the mountain was again burning low. The piper shuddered, looking at it, and drew the last husband's jacket closer round himself.

To the woman, the fairground looked not at all like the ones she had seen pictured in brightly illustrated children's books: carousels with brightly painted wooden horses that went up and down, up and down, big wheels which swung you high into the air so that you could see far across the city, roller coasters that climbed slowly and then dipped dizzyingly until you screamed with the pleasure of it all. This place was more like a shanty town — she had seen pictures of shanty-towns in newspapers and magazines: home-made tents of curtaining and sheeting, huts made of cardboard boxes with crudely drawn signs on them. Oil lanterns hung around these edifices emitting a wavering yellow light. A small crowd of poorly dressed people, mostly, she surmised, from the flats, wandered listlessly amid the squalor, buying violently orange fizzy drinks or dusty candy-floss that burnt the tongue and coated the teeth, or hot dogs on buns soggy with wet onion and ketchup. Dirty, barefoot children took rides on a broken-down old nag, six at a time, screeching and pulling on its poor mangy mane.

The piper dragged her past, though she scanned the children's faces intently. They stopped outside an orange tent with a sign in red paint: **BEARDED LADY**.

A dwarf stood outside, ringing a bell.

"Roll up," he shouted in a voice that was amazingly deep for such a little fellow, "Roll up and see the amazin bearded lady. Guaranteed genuwine. Give it a pull if you don't believe me."

A small crowd had gathered and there was some laughter.

"Give what a pull?" shouted a red-faced woman in the crowd, provoking coarse shrieks.

"How do we know it aint a feller?" shouted a man in a cap at her side.

The dwarf riposted, "With them tits, you kiddin me!"

The audience laughed again, appreciatively.

"Heard of the Hairy Ainus, sirs and madams?" the dwarf inquired. "No? Wherever was you brought up? Well, anyway, this lady, sirs and madams, is a genuwine authentic Hairy Ainu, come all the way from Japan for your delectification."

The crowd was starting to look bored and beginning to drift away.

"Well," the dwarf shouted in his deep voice, "if the bearded lady don't grab you, what about the limbless man?"

The crowd turned back at this.

"Two for the price of one, sirs and madams. An offer you can't refuse. The bearded lady AND the limbless man under one mind-bogglin roof."

The crowd pushed forward eagerly, pressing coins into the dwarf's cap, which he held out for the purpose. The piper made to go in, too. The woman held back.

"Come on," he persisted. "At least you'll be able to sit down for a few minutes."

The woman's back and legs were aching again. She had even staggered a few times, so the piper's argument convinced her. It was also very cheap to see the show: a few pennies each satisfied the dwarf.

Inside the tent, the light seemed orange because of the vividness of the tent-cloth. After a few moments, during which the crowd started to get restless, the dwarf leapt on to a slightly raised dais at one end of the tent.

"And now," he uttered, "the moment you all been waitin for: Madama Butterfly, the bearded lady from Japan."

He applauded wildly, accompanied by a few half-hearted claps from the audience.

A stout woman, not looking in the slightest degree Japanese entered wearing a kimono and holding a large fan coyly in front of her face. She walked crab-wise across the dais and then suddenly lowered the fan. The audience gasped at the length and bushiness of her auburn beard. Then the red-faced woman shouted, "I still think it's a man."

The bearded lady regarded the red-faced woman for a moment with scorn. Then she started taking off her kimono. Underneath there was another, and under that another. It was like the children's party game of pass the parcel where a huge parcel ends up as a small package. Discarded kimonos soon covered the dais in a rag-heap of colour.

The audience was chanting, "More, more, more."

The bearded lady paused. She had reached the last garment. The audience fell silent. Man or woman - they would soon know. Suddenly, they became aware of something else on the dais. The heaped kimonos started to heave and wriggle. Somehow, unseen by the audience, the limbless man had got in under them. His bald head finally came up through the robes like a worm in a flower garden. The audience gasped again. The limbless man was no more than a metre long, head and torso enclosed in a sack that tied round his neck. No arms, no legs. There was at least no possibility that this could be a trick.

The bearded lady, meanwhile, swept away the kimonos and knelt on the dais, like a geisha girl. The limbless man wriggled over to her and with his teeth seized the ribbon holding her last robe together. In a few swift jerks he had it undone. She extended her arms and he pulled the kimono from her, this time slowly, slowly. She crouched there, now naked, except for a G-string. One arm brushed way the beard that covered her chests. Pendulous breasts hung there for all to see.

"More," hissed the red-faced woman. "We've all seen old men with tits. More."

The bearded lady looked hard at the red-faced woman again as if to memorise her face. She nodded to the limbless man. He pulled the tie of the G-string in his teeth. The audience made no sound. He took the G-string away in his mouth, like a dog, then dropped it, licking his lips. The audience laughed.

The bearded woman stood up. Her undoubtedly female crotch was completely hairless. Slowly, and with dignity, she walked naked from the tent, to the wild applause of the audience. Some even threw more coins on to the stage. The limbless man picked them up with his tongue and deposited them in the dwarf's cap. The dexterity with which he did this caused more and more coins to be thrown. It was worth every penny to see his wriggling body, his curling tongue. The dwarf clapped too.

"How about that? How about that?"

He was hopping and leaping, clearly delighted with the success of the show.

The piper clapped enthusiastically with the rest. Only the woman sat not moving, a faint expression of disgust on her face. She was staring in horrible fascination at the limbless man who was now organising himself a smoke, manipulating cigarette, match and matchbox with his incredibly long and muscular pink tongue.

The woman got up abruptly, pulling the piper by the hand.

"Why did you bring me here?" she whispered loudly. "My daughter couldn't possibly be here. These people are nothing but FREAKS."

The room had gone quiet and her last words were clearly audible. The dwarf, the limbless man, everyone suddenly looked at her.

"Admittedly," the piper said softly, "some of them don't look like you or me. But you know, they behave with immense dignity and respect towards each other."

The woman curled her lip. "So?"

"What I mean is, many of those you might consider normal," the piper was floundering, his hand instinctively reaching for his tin whistle. He hated making speeches, "many of those you might even consider attractive," (a middle-aged bejewelled woman in an expensive fur coat had entered the tent and was approaching the dwarf) "many who are apparently charming in every way," (the bejewelled woman was whispering now to the dwarf) "conceal under such flawless exteriors minds of the most horrible ugliness and depravity," (the bejewelled woman let herself be led backstage by the dwarf, who paused merely to have a word with the limbless man) "whereas with these people what you think of as their ugliness is all on the outside, for the world to see!" (the limbless man slithered backstage after the bejewelled woman and the dwarf) "while inside they are pure and beautiful."

The dwarf came from the backstage area rubbing his hands. He crossed to the piper.

"My dear sir," he exclaimed exuberantly, "how utterly delightful to see you again. And lookin, if I might make so bold, so dapper!"

He rubbed the cloth of the last husband's jacket appreciatively between two stubby fingers.

"And the little lady," the dwarf went on, his pale eyes almost twinkling, "who thinks we're all freaks."

The woman was embarrassed.

"I didn't mean it as an insult," she babbled. "It's just that I'm looking for my daughter who's lost and the piper said she might be here and now I can't imagine why he thinks she might be because... because..."

"Because she looks quite normal," the dwarf went on, chuckling. "Of course she do. But madam," he bowed low, "you have just enjoyed the rare privilege of seeing two of the most unusual of our performers. The cream de la cream, as they say in la belle France, so to speak. Howsoever and nevertheless, many of our midgets are perfectly normal in appearance, only being built on a smaller scale than what you are. And one or two of our performers, when out of costume, of course, and in their civvies, could not be distinguished in any way in a crowd of your normal people. I'd lay a wager on it, I would."

The dwarf put his finger on his nose in a meaningful gesture.

"For example, our strong man, though endowed with an exceptional well-developed body, would pass for an insurance clerk or bus conductor in a suit or uniform. Our lady contortionist, though capable of puttin the toe of her right foot in at her left ear, at the same time puttin her left toe over the top of her head and up her left nostril, would look quite at ease in any Eye-talian mode you might pick out of any classy fashion magazine. As for our latest exhibit, the Sleepin Beauty or as we prefer to call her, Snow White and the four dwarfs, she is pretty as the proverbial picture."

"Snow White?" the piper said. "That's one of yours I haven't seen yet."

"Well," the dwarf commented, "you wouldn't have, would you. I meantersay, we have only acquired her recent. At great expense, I might add," he winked.

"Excuse me a moment," he went on, as a small middle-aged man in a fur jacket approached him. They stepped away together and a discussion ensued. Meanwhile the woman looked at the piper.

"I don't suppose this Sleeping Beauty could be my daughter."

"It's worth checking out," he answered. "I'll ask Mishka."

The dwarf had led the middle-aged man in the fur jacket to the side of the tent where a small tear in the fabric enabled him, crouching, to peer inside. The dwarf left him there and returned to the piper, tossing a silver coin in his hand.

"You call us freaks," he said to the woman. "What about them, then? Pillars of society! He's some bigwig, an alderman, pots of money. The woman with jewels and fur coat what you might of noticed earlier, that's his lady wife. She comes secretly every week to be… ahem… attended to, so to speak, by the limbless man, if you get my meaning, sir and madam. That's how she gets her kicks. Secretly, every week, her husband follows her and spies on them. And that's how he gets his. Pillars of society, how's yer father! No, madam, my point is, who are the freaks?" he finished triumphantly. "Who, eh? Who?"

"But you," the woman said, "accommodate them."

"Ah yes, well, a purely business transaction," the dwarf replied, juggling coins in the air adroitly. "Both sides pay handsomely. And we need the money."

"And the limbless man?" the woman began.

"Madam, you would be surprised at how many ladies, highly respectable ladies at that, appreciate his services. You saw him out there today. What any other man needs hands, feet and other appendages for, he does with his lips, teeth and tongue. Better," the dwarf added significantly, rubbing his large nose again.

The woman turned away again in disgust.

"Could we see your Snow White?" the piper asked. "She sounds intriguing."

"Show's about to begin," the dwarf said. "Follow me."

They crossed the wasteland, the dwarf holding an oil lamp as high as he could, notwithstanding which the woman stumbled at times over blocks of concrete or into deep craters.

Behind them, the once furred and bejewelled woman sank in naked ecstasy on the filthy floor of the tent, every inch of her skin licked over by the rough pink tongue of the limbless Man, while outside, trembling and sweating, her husband yearned and silently wept.

Waiting

The masked and helmeted policeman waited. The light in the woman protester's room went out. He waited, the glow from a distant bonfire turning his helmet dark purple.

Burning

The singer stood under a cool shower. She had been standing there for a long time, her black hair loose to the ground, clinging to her like the robe of an arab woman. Her heavy eyes were closed. She opened her mouth and drank in the cool water. Still she burned. The fire would not go out.

The crack in the paving stones

The old crone shuffled down the dark alleyway that led to her basement room. She had fish for her cats. The fish stank a little but the cats wouldn't mind. They would probably enjoy it all the more. The trouble was, she could hardly see. Her eyes were not the best and she never usually went out in the dark. Now it was inexplicably dark all the time. No matter when she woke up, it was dark. She had gone to the police station meaning to ask. She wanted to tell them of the other matter and then, just at the end of the conversation, she had been planning to ask what had happened to the sun. To ask humbly in case they laughed at her. For she was afraid it might just be dark for her. And that everyone else would know it was dark just for her and would laugh. It was a fearful thing to grow old and not to know anything.

Of course, she hadn't asked. She hadn't even reached the desk of the duty officer. She had been too afraid. And now here she was home again at last. She knew this because she had so often counted how many steps it took from the corner of her street: fifty-seven. Then she felt the uneven crack in the paving stones that told her she was right outside her basement room. She felt along the railings until her fingers reached the gate. It was open. That was unusual. She was always careful to close it. It must be those lads again! Those lads who crept down into the darkness outside her room and smoked their funny cigarettes and stuck their needles into themselves and left the needles lying about. The lads she had wanted to complain about. She thought she could hear their suppressed breathing. She felt her way carefully down the metal stairs to her basement room where her hungry cats were waiting. Perhaps the lads knew that she had been to complain. She trembled and nearly slipped. She reached her front door and fiddled with her keys. She dropped them. She groped in the garbage heaped outside her door. Her hand touched something furry and stiff. She retrieved the keys but lifted the stiff thing. Perhaps it was a rat. She hoped it was a rat. She opened her door and went in and locked the door behind her. She lit a dim lamp and for a moment was relieved that she could see clearly again. Then she wished she couldn't see at all, for the soft stiff thing she was holding was her dear cat, Francis, and he was dead, his poor neck broken. And stuffed inside the pretty little collar that she had bought for his sixth birthday, inside the pretty little collar round his poor broken neck was a crudely scribbled note: **KEP YOR MOUT SHUT OR YOR NEX.**

Dazzler

The Commissioner felt nice and full. He had finished his dessert. It couldn't have been more delightful. The protester who looked like Jesus had behaved like Judas and shopped all his mates. After a few prods, it was true, but the Commissioner felt he should have been able to withstand a lot more. The few prods inflicted on the protester who looked like Jesus were chicken feed compared to what had been done to some of his predecessors in the interview room. But the Commissioner was delighted about this for he was actually squeamish about inflicting prods beyond the call of duty. He enjoyed the moral victory far more. The way the protester who looked like Jesus had crawled on his hands and knees in his own vomit, shit and blood to lick the shoes of the Commissioner — craving his pardon for having been rude to him earlier in the day and for vomiting the entire contents of his guts and more, then proceeding to vomit the names of everyone he knew in any organisation of a protesting nature — that was what gave the Commissioner the greatest sense of repletion. He foresaw a commendation for himself. They would be dazzled by his success. The little matter of El Blanco was nothing compared to this.

The breast

The masked and helmeted figure had used his skeleton keys to enter the room of the woman protester. He stared at her sleeping body, the child asleep beside her, its hand gripping her ear. A dim glow from a bonfire in the street outside faintly illuminated the room. His eyes were already used to the dark and he gazed at the woman. One side of her face was purple and swollen from where he had hit her earlier. The masked and helmeted cop hadn't realised that he had hit her so hard. Probably she bruised easily. He hoped she realised that he had hit her for her own good, to protect her. When he had picked her up, she had felt so soft, so soft.

The woman stirred in her sleep and moaned. As she turned over, she flung out an arm exposing a naked breast. He stared at it in shock. She went to bed naked! The breast was full and pale, blue-veined with a large dark nipple, the breast of a mother who suckled her children long. He stood still as a statue, staring at the breast, gently rising, gently falling.

With a kiss

The tent where Snow White was to be shown was of dark blue material. The light falling through it from street lamps beyond seemed phosphorescent. Inside the tent there was only an oil lamp held aloft by the dwarf and flinging distorted shadows over his already twisted features. A thin crowd fidgeted and shivered and called for the show to begin. Suddenly, the dwarf shone his lamp at the rear of the tent where a rough black curtain was hanging.

"She's behind there," he whispered hoarsely. "She's behind there, sleepin. Ladies and gents, you are about to be privileged to see one of the true wonders of the world. A bee-yutiful demwoselle plunged into the deepest sleep that comes before death. Plunged, I say, into this deep slumber for five long years..."

"I thought he said she was their newest exhibit," the woman whispered to the piper.

"Shh. That's just showman's patter."

"Step right up, ladies and gents," the dwarf was continuing, "and observe this marvel where she lies."

With a dramatic sweep of his arm, he pulled aside the curtain to reveal a young girl lying on a low couch. A loud "ooh" came from the audience. Snow White was indeed astonishingly beautiful. Dark red hair lay in heaps round her shoulders. Her skin was creamy white, her lips coral. She looked as perfect and as unreal as a waxwork.

"Step up, ladies and gents," the dwarf said again. "prove to your own satisfaction that this here aint no doll, no corpse, but a livin breathin woman."

The crowd pushed forward, the woman and piper among them.

"Aint she lovely, ladies and gents?" the dwarf purred, holding the flickering lamp over the motionless body. "Pretty as the proverbial picture, you might say. I could just stand and stare at her for hours, I could. Do she dream? What do you think? Do she await her hansom prince? Yes, you may touch her, sir."

A man poked Snow White tentatively, getting no response. The crowd pushed on in to her then, poking, pinching, clapping loudly in her ear. One man boldly cupped his hand over her small, round breast.

"No, no, not there sir," remonstrated the dwarf in mock severity. "Show some respect."

"I was only trying to feel her heartbeat," the man insisted, to knowing jeers from the crowd.

"She aint wax, is she sir. She'd warm and soft. But you won't waken her. We tried everythin." The dwarf ushered back the crowd, waving the lamp in their flushed and eager faces. "Step back now, ladies and gents. Take your seats please, so that everyone can observe the demonstration."

The woman turned to the piper, who was staring fixedly at Snow White.

"Is she really asleep or is it a fake?" she asked him.

"I don't know."

A woman in the crowd shouted up, "How does she eat?"

The dwarf bowed at her.

"A good question, madam. An excellent question. That and even more intimate services are left to us, her

faithful and lovin servants." There were again knowing and suggestive oohs from the red-faced and sweating crowd. "A lady midget, I might add, performs those duties I would blush to mention in mixed company."

"Oh-ho!"

"Yeah, right."

"By means of a tube down her throat, we twice daily admit of sustenance."

"Ugh!"

"Yuk!"

"Disgusting!"

The dwarf suddenly clapped his hands and shouted "Rodolpho!"

To gasps from the crowd, a tiny deformed creature entered wearing an outsize purple turban fastened with a gigantic gilt brooch. He was playing inexpertly upon bagpipes. The dwarf put down his lamp and picked up a drum. Together they marched round the couch, the dwarf banging as ear-splittingly as he could, the midget producing excruciating wails from the bagpipes. The lamp on the floor threw giant shadows on to the back of the tent.

The audience screamed and covered its ears but Snow White did not so much as stir or sigh.

"Ain't that a sound to waken the dead, ladies and gents?" bawled the dwarf on top of everything else. "But she don't hear it. So what about this then?" He drew from Rodolpho's turban a long thin hat pin with a large cloudy bead at one end. "Examine it please, ladies and gents. Note the acute sharpness of the tip, madam." And grabbing a woman's hand, jabbed the pin into her finger. She yelped as everyone else laughed loudly. "Oh, excuse me, I'm sure... Here. let me suck it better for you." The woman drew back while the crowd fell to pieces with laughter.

"Just to prove, ladies and gents, that a mere touch draws blood. Now observe if you please."

The dwarf once again approached the recumbent Snow White, still as marble. He raised one white hand to his mouth and kissed it. Then, with a violent gesture, he appeared to drive the pin right through the hand. The crowd gasped again. The piper winced as if in pain and clenched his own hand.

"Not only don't she react," the dwarf was saying, "she don't bleed neither. Come up here, sir, and check what I say is true. Yes, you sir." He was looking directly at the piper.

Still clenching his hand, the piper walked warily up to Snow White. Carefully, carefully, he took her white hand in his. He turned it tenderly and examined how the cloud-tipped pin went right through the middle of the palm without drawing a single drop of blood. Yet the hand was soft and warm. He nodded back at the audience.

"Yes, she's alive alive-o awright," the dwarf was saying, his eyes now fixed on the besotted piper, who was still holding Snow White's hand. The dwarf took it from him, drew out the hat pin and laid the hand back on the exhibit's breast. "She aint no corpse, she aint no doll. See her sweet boo-soom rises and falls with the regularity of a sleeping babe. Hold a mirror before her mouth and see how her breath clouds it."

He handed the piper a mirror. The piper put it near those slightly parted lips. The faintest veil covered the mirror for a second and was gone. Again it came, and again was gone. The piper again nodded at the now silent audience.

The dwarf was still gazing at the piper.

"I know you to be a man of sensitivity, sir. An artist. Do you agree that what I say is true?"

Very low: "It is true."

"Speak up sir, no one can hear you."

Slightly louder: "It is true."

"Thank you, sir."

"There is no doubt, ladies and gents," the dwarf continued in ringing tones, "But that she awaits her hansom prince. No sir, it aint you," he said to the piper, still standing awkwardly next to Snow White. "You can sit down again if your honour pleases. And try to get a control on yourself."

The piper made his way back to his seat amid titters from the audience. The woman looked at him wondering.

"Yes, ladies and gents, Snow White awaits her hansom prince. And lo! he comes...."

The dwarf beat a roll on his drum and stood expectantly. Nothing happened.

"God Almighty!" he shouted, "Is he deaf?" He peered into the recesses of the tent and shouted again. "Yes, cloth-ears, I'm talking to you. Ready now, are you? Right." The dwarf assumed an attitude again and beat another roll on his drum. "And lo! he comes." He put his hand to his ear. "He comes. He comes."

A fiendishly ugly and lopsided midget came lolloping on to the stage astride a broom with its tufted head uppermost. The audience again collapsed in laughter.

"Behold," the dwarf shouted, "Sir Gallyhad!"

The dwarf then struck the midget, who fell to the floor under the force from the blow.

"Don't miss your cue next time," he said as the ugly midget scrabbled to get up, "or I'll cut off your privileges."

The sight of the ugly midget endeavouring with great difficulty to get back up, burdened as he was both with a hump and with the broom-horse, sent the audience into further uncontrolled convulsions, augmented by the grotesquely rolling eyes of the little creature.

"Can this be he?" exclaimed the dwarf. "What do you think, lady?" He singled out the woman who was cringing in her seat next to the piper, and fixed her with a malevolent stare. "Can the kiss of this... what would you like to call him, this... freak awaken our Snow White? Wouldn't you wake up if he gave you a kiss?" He came right up to the woman and put his long white face down close to hers. "Wouldn't you just, eh? You'd pretend it was a nightmare, wouldn't you. I'll bet you'd turn over and go back to sleep pretty sharpish, wouldn't you. Eh?"

The woman could smell the dwarf's breath, so close to her. Amazingly, it was light and sweet, as if perfumed with flowers. If she shut her eyes, perhaps she could take herself back to the rose garden. Perhaps then the nightmare would go away. She shut her eyes but an icy blast blew in her face and the roses went brown and withered.

The dwarf had moved away.

"What we have to remember, ladies and gents, is that there aint no accountin for taste. Remember Beauty and the Beast. Maybe, just maybe, Snow White here would consider our Sir Gallyhad the sexiest hunk she could hope for. Let's see, ladies and gents. Let's see if his kiss can awaken her. The moment you've all been waitin for, ladies and gents."

He beat another roll on his drum. Rodolpho, standing all the while patiently to one side, let out an ear-splitting blast on his bagpipes. The ugly midget bowed grotesquely. He hovered over Snow White's face for a moment. Then turned to the audience and shook his head.

"Whaddyamean?" the dwarf asked him threateningly. "You don't fancy it? Not ugly enough for you, is she?"

The ugly midget whispered in the dwarf's ear. The dwarf nodded knowingly.

"Oh, I see," he said. "I see, yes, yes, I see, I see."

This went on for some time until the audience started to get restive.

The dwarf whispered confidentially.

"He's very disappointed. He was expecting the Bearded Lady. This one just aint hairy enough for him... Like what I said, there's no accountin for tastes. OK," the dwarf announced suddenly, "if it's the Bearded Lady you want, a Bearded Lady you shall have."

He whipped up Snow White's skirt and the midget crawled underneath, wriggling and grunting obscenely. The audience cheered wildly.

"The kiss of life, ladies and gents," the dwarf yelled. "She wakes, she wakes! Does she, does she not?"

The piper seized the woman by the hand and rushed from the tent. His face was streaming with tears.

The woman spat at him. "Friends of your, are they. What does that make you, then? It's disgusting." The piper held his head in his hands in despair.

"Deformed minds in deformed bodies, if you ask me." Screams of laughter could still be heard from the tent. The piper ran further off.

"Moral dignity, heh?" the woman snapped, following him. "Respect towards each other. Loyalty. That's what you said."

"No." the piper wept.

"Yes you did."

"No, I mean I don't believe they were doing what... it looked like they were doing."

Laughter, waves on waves of it, still washed over them.

"Sounds like they're doing something even worse now. Perhaps you'd like to go back in and see."

"All it shows," the piper said, trying hard, "is the extreme disgust and scorn they feel for their audience. For us. Don't you see that?"

"No."

"Freaks we call them," the piper went on. "You called them that yourself. Hide them away, cast them out, they have no place in nice society. But perhaps after all it's us they should cast out." The roars of laughter continued. The piper would have liked to drown. "Listen to that crowd," he said. "Listen to those nice normal respectable people in there. Those family men and women. Pillars of society. So who are the real freaks, I ask you? Who?"

The woman looked at his agonised face.

"At any rate," she commented, "my daughter isn't here."

"Then let us leave," the piper said.

They stumbled across the site, this time unaided by the dwarf's oil lamp, clutching each other to avoid falling into craters. So intent were they on their safe passage, they failed to notice the hunched-up figure of a middle-aged man in an expensive jacket lying in the mud and sobbing. They failed to see, having passed the orange tent, the middle-aged woman, without most of her jewels but wearing again her coat — though as it swung open there was now evidently nothing under it — emerge from the back of the tent rubbing her genitalia in ecstasy with her furry sleeve. She too tottered off across the site, passing but not seeing — for love is blind — the hunched-up figure of her husband. Had the piper and the woman entered the orange tent a few moments later they would have found the bearded lady cavorting around in the peachy silk underwear of the middle-aged lady, diamonds dripping from her ears, a gold charm bracelet tied round her narrow ankles and a ruby necklace flashing fire around her thin waist.

In the bearded lady's hand was a little red-faced doll. The bearded lady, as she danced and cavorted, was sewing up the doll's gash of a mouth with thick brown thread. She laughed, a high-pitched tinkle of a laugh as she danced and sewed, and the jewels jingle-jangled an accompaniment.

Beneath her, reclining on the dais amid the bright kimonos, was the limbless man, smooth as a slug, naked and white and glistening. The bearded lady flung the sewn-up doll away, lit herself a cigarette, paused to take a few drags and then, laughing her jingling laugh, put the cigarette into the limbless man's pink mouth.

A few moments before, back in the blue tent, the red-faced woman had been howling with the rest, urging on the ugly midget to further obscenities. She was screeching with laughter, clutching her flabby breasts and swigging from time to time from a flask of home-made gin that hung around her thick neck. Suddenly, in mid-screech, her jaws locked hard. She grabbed her throat, she tried to force her fingers into her mouth, her face went redder and redder in the attempt. The crowd around her laughed heartily at the way her face contorted. Almost as good as the show! Suddenly the red-faced woman, her lips sealed, flew through the air across the room and landed in a heap in the corner. The audience exploded into applause. Only the dwarf, looking concerned, crossed hurriedly to where she lay. The red-face woman looked up at him trembling.

"You shouldn't oughter have done it," he said, shaking his head. "She's awful touchy. You shouldn't oughter have done it. Go home. I'll see what can be done. Go home and don't never come back."

The audience, it's attention again focussed on the doings on the dais did not see the red-faced woman drag her bruised body out of the blue tent, across the craters and crevices of the bombed site to one of the towering flats. No one saw her drag herself up the stairs to her filthy room. And when later she was able to open her mouth a crack — had the dwarf said a word? had a stitch gone loose? — no one saw how much home-made gin she poured through it until a blessed unconsciousness overcame her and she sank into sleep amid the potato peelings and discarded cabbage leaves of her life.

Cold fire

The singer was back in the bar, singing. A few customers had drifted in despite the continuous presence of the dead tourist outside. By now they were getting used to him. They drank alone and silently, hardly paying any attention to the singer's throaty song. But when she stopped, they clapped and asked for more. Anything to fill the silence. She shut her heavy eyes and sang of heartbreak and despair, of hard times, hard times, and no way out. Despite the heat in the bar, her body burned no longer. A cold sweat covered her, she felt pearls of it gather under her armpits and trickle down her skin.

Outside on the chill mountain, shadowy figures huddled round the embers of the bonfire, occasionally throwing something on to it to prevent it going out completely. They gazed trancelike as twigs first sizzled, then flared, then subsided into the fire's scarlet heart. People from the city staggered up from time to time with offerings, like pilgrims or pagans. One man emptied half a bottle of brandy on the pyre, which flared for a few blue seconds, then died back again. The shadowy figures watched him with smoke-dulled eyes. The man collapsed in an alcoholic stupor.

Soon, soon, they would strip him and burn his clothes. Later, maybe, they would burn him, too.

The pimp in the turquoise shirt waxes philosophical

Down in the Street of Innocents business was brisk. Nothing like an apocalypse to bring on the need for a good screw. The fat whore in the bikini and black see-through blouse could never remember being so much in demand. She had hardly turned one trick when the next client came in. She had hardly time to fix her bikini on again and sometimes just slipped into the blouse or even just covered her private parts with the ever more soiled sheet.

The pimp in the turquoise shirt and green silk trousers opined to himself that in times of trouble fat women were at a premium because along with sex they provided comfort, reminding the punters of their mothers, perhaps. The pimp in the turquoise shirt, who considered himself something of a philosopher, made a mental note to get in more of the meaty ones. Easier said, however, than done. The drugs they took soon made them skinny as skeletons. Mind you, the kids — boys and girls alike — were also much in demand. Scruples go out the window when the end of the world is nigh. Though as far as the end of the world went, the philosopher pimp had his doubts. Hadn't he seen it all before? Hadn't the signs all been there? Hadn't the same predictions been made? Yet here everyone, or almost everyone, still was. Pity about the new kid with the ruptured spleen. He might have known that old bird was a kink. Just to look at his drooling mouth, his runny red eyes, his saggy neck. He, the pimp, with his vast experience, should have known the old bird wasn't kosher. And that new kid! He'd had great expectations of her. Like a little fairy on top of the Christmas tree, she was. Pretty as a little picture. He'd have cleaned up with her on an endless night like this. The philosopher pimp spat a gob of green phlegm into the gutter.

The last laugh

The Commissioner was in a cold sweat. He had hardly any appetite for the apple strudel with whipped cream on his desk, while the hot chocolate drink was growing a thick skin. Fuck the bastard! Fuck him!

First, the bastard had given him completely wrong information. All those names — made up, every last one of them. All those addresses, non-existent or, if they existed, inhabited by worthy and respectable pillars of the community. Oh, they had been rounded up all right, they had been brought in, dragged through doors which had been kicked in, through smashed windows. But the Commissioner knew that he would have to let the lot of them go. And then there would be complaints. Pillars of the community were always very assiduous about sending in complaints.

But that wasn't the worst of it. When he had finally stormed down to the cells to kick the shit out of the lying bastard, the bugger was already dead, lying quiet and more Christ-like than ever in the corner of his cell. None of the other fuckers had even noticed. The bugger had died of a punctured lung or something, silently and unnoticed in the corner of a crowded cell. Sure the Commissioner had beaten the shit out of the other inmates, but where had that got him? Precisely nowhere. Those bastards knew nothing. The Commissioner bit sorrowfully into his strudel. Cream and apple chunks dropped on to his lap. He cursed, he had no luck. They'd throw the book at him over this for sure.

He remembered looking down at the bastard in disbelief (scraping the apple and cream off his trousers with podgy fingers and licking them). He had even kicked the body. Then, when the Christ-like and lifeless face had slipped on to the floor, he had kicked him even more, not meaning to, but just unable to stop. The guy had been laughing at him all along. The guy had been laughing at him and now death had the last laugh.

The Commissioner drank a draught of lukewarm chocolate and didn't even notice the skin that remained hanging over his top lip.

Trust me

The amateur artist had known that the man in the corner was dead. He had been dead for some time. She thought she had even noticed when the repressed twitches of agony had stopped at last. She had said nothing to the Commissioner when he slapped her across the face, when he kicked her in the belly. Why should she do him any favours? Now she sketched on a scrap of paper the Christ-like face of the dead protester in front of her. She sketched his noble features, his long curls, the blood that trickled from the side of his mouth. When she was finished to her satisfaction, she kissed his already cool forehead and whispered into his ear, "You can trust me. I'll remember. I'll pass on the message."

Then she kissed his lips and drank down the blood on his mouth.

How wrong can you be

It was the smell first. She knew he was there from the smell. She didn't open her eyes nor let a twitch betray her, imagining that his shaded eyes were fixed on her face (actually they were still fixed on her exposed breast). She had been thinking hard for some time, not sure what it meant. Had he sussed her? She thought not or he would have dragged her back by the hair to the cells. He was here for himself. She would have known precisely what to do if it weren't for the child. The child was a problem. The child was at risk. Still, she would have to risk it. There was no other way. She twisted herself as if still asleep and hot, so hot. She flung off the cover from her body so that it covered the child completely. That was something, anyway, and the child had barely stirred. She lay on her back, her legs slightly apart, and waited.

Nothing happened. Perhaps after all he only wanted to look. But that seemed unlikely.

The masked and armoured cop stared at the woman's broad nakedness. She was apparently asleep. Her eyes were closed and she was breathing regularly. He had thought this time that he wouldn't hit her. There had been too much of that already. But now, looking at the broad nakedness of her, like a soft Renoir nude (the cop liked to think of himself as a man of culture), he had the deepest desire again to pummel this one black and blue like the others, to tear out her hair, to break her teeth. The stink off him grew stronger, although he didn't notice it. Suddenly she opened her eyes and stared right at him. Now she will scream, he thought, and I will beat her to death. But she didn't scream. She kept cold eyes fixed on him. For once he was unnerved. He could almost smell himself now. He took off his gauntlets and lightly touched the hair at her crotch. It was soft and damp. He felt her. He suddenly wanted to bury his arm in her, up to the elbow. He wanted to hear her call to him. But she just looked at him with that cold fixed expression, and he began for some reason to tear off his clothes. He would leave his mask on: then she wouldn't see his face. Then he wouldn't have to kill her. Not unless he wanted to. Now he didn't know whether he wanted to or not. He would kill her, he thought, if she could tell that he had never screwed a warm living woman before. If he could see from her face that she had somehow guessed his secret. He was hard now. Almost as hard as he had been those other times. She was still staring coldly and emotionlessly at him. He plunged himself into her at the same moment that she, reaching under her pillow, drew out a small gun and fired it close and soundlessly into his chest. As his heart's blood gushed on to her broad body, he stared at her cold hard face, and knew in his last second just how wrong he had been.

Blood

The Commissioner's wife had several hobbies. One was flower arranging. Once she had even come second in a local competition and another time had been highly commended. She generally took a theme to inspire her. Today, before the darkness had enveloped the city, she had sent a maid to the square and the maid had come back with an armful of yellow, orange, gold and red flowers that had left a powder of pollen over her black hair. Now the Commissioner's wife was busy spiking the blooms in an elaborate design that represented a highly stylised sun. She would be holding a dinner party that endless night after the concert and was rather pleased with herself for thinking up the sun motif. It should go down a bomb, she thought.

As she worked, she ran through in her head the schedule for the evening. Everything was in order. She had after all done this so many times before that the organising was automatic. In one more hour she would have finished the flower arrangement, for, as a second prize-winner, she knew the value of taking one's time and not rushing. Over the next hour she would visit the kitchen, to make sure there were no last minute hitches. She would inspect the banqueting hall, as she referred to her rather large dining room, to ascertain that all was in order there too, that the place names were correctly positioned on the tables, along with an appropriate small gift for each guest. The Commissioner's wife's great talent, and one which she prided herself on, was her ability to delegate when necessary, as well as her attention to the smallest detail.

When she was certain that all was running smoothly, she would take herself off to her own suite, where her personal maid would run an aromatic bath for her. She would soak herself for fifteen minutes, would then dry herself and allow her maid to oil her all over — for age, and many baths, and much sun-bathing at luxury resorts, had dried her skin into leathery wrinkles. Then she would fit herself into the magenta gown with the plunging neckline that she had chosen for the evening, and place around her neck and hang from her ears the jewellery of spiky jet that was an inspired choice of accessory. While in the best taste and evidently expensive, the jewellery nonetheless had a punkish quality appropriate for the rock concert she would be attending earlier in the evening. Once she was attired, perfumed and made-up — and the application of her make-up

in itself took over an hour — once her hair was done — ever so slightly spiked and sprayed with faint purple in another concession to the occasion — she would have to go and check on the Commissioner. She sighed at the thought. That was the least pleasurable of the preparations. Still, she had given the most careful instructions to the Commissioner's personal valet, a man she had picked herself and in whom she placed the most absolute trust. She could rest assured that at the start of the evening at least the Commissioner would present a spotless and flawless exterior. Whatever happened thereafter would be neither her fault nor the valet's. The valet! A man indeed of the greatest discretion. She smiled a carnivorous smile as she spiked a lemon-coloured dahlia, and her yellow eyes glinted. Gentlemen, she thought to herself, should beware what they say in confidence to their valets when those valets have been handpicked by their wives. How the Commissioner would rage and splutter — ineffectually of course — if he only knew what confidences his valet had betrayed to his wife in the privacy of the wife's suite while the Commissioner was at work! The valet adored her, of course, but she firmly believed in keeping such people in their place. Let him watch her, if he wished, perform her toilette. God knew, for a woman of her age she still had a remarkable figure and wasn't ashamed of her naked body. If the sanctioned glimpses of it caused the valet to creep in to her regularly with new indiscretions on the part of the Commissioner, so much the better.

Suddenly, she let out a little scream and a word that in polite society she would never have uttered: she had spiked her forefinger. She watched transfixed as drops of her blood continued to fall on to the half-finished flower arrangement, until a maid rushed over to her with a disinfectant swab and a sticking plaster. She waved the sticking plaster away in disgust until she suddenly remembered that bandages and plasters were a feature of the costumes of The Martyrdom of St Sebastian, and realised what a brilliant touch it would be to sport not just this one of necessity but several more on exposed parts of her body.

The beads of blood had settled on the flower arrangement like tiny rubies. She would leave them there.

Feasts

In the city square, small creatures were busy at the body of the dead tourist. They were having the feast of their lives.

Down a dark alley, in a basement, similar small creatures were sniffing at four prostrate bodies and tentatively nibbling at fingers and ears. But these bodies were still warm, though perhaps not for much longer, and blood still coursed, if sluggishly now, through their veins. Inside a basement flat, doors and windows bolted, huddled the old crone, clutching her dead Francis and waiting for morning.

Bang Bang Bang Bang

The woman was striding purposefully into the square, the piper behind her now, trying to catch at her sleeve to hold her back.

"Haven't you learnt anything yet?" the piper said to her. "You won't get any help there."

The woman looked at him with blindly stubborn eyes.

"I still trust the system," she told him, "despite what you say."

"One of these days you're in for a nasty shock."

The woman was feeling cruel.

"Well, no one else," she said, " has so far done anything for me."

She entered the police station — there was no queue now — and climbed to the upper level. The piper took his customary position under a tree and began to play softly. The mother with the pram crossed the square, not pausing and not looking at him. In the bar, the singer, soothing her rough throat with yet another glass of warm red wine, caught the evocative notes of the pipe and began to burn again. In a cell below ground, the amateur artist whispered names to herself over and over, singing them to the piper's tune to help her remember.

The woman climbed the stairs to the desk where the officer sat surrounded with heaps of paper. Another stood to one side, banging his baton off his hand.

The officer at the desk did not look up at the woman.

"Petitioning time is in the mornings," he said.

"I was here in the morning," the woman replied, thinking that she had no idea what time of the day it now was. "I just wondered if there was any news."

"None," the officer said, not looking up.

"You've found no one answering my daughter's description?" the woman persisted.

"No."

"Are you sure? Could you check again?"

"She's with her granny in Ballydehob," the standing officer said with a grin.

The woman turned on him. "Oh, so you think it's funny. My problem is of no importance to you. The fate of my daughter holds no interest. Well, let me ask you if you've even checked whether she was not one of those abducted by the Commissioner's very good friend, Mr El Blanco?"

Both officers started, the standing one ceasing abruptly to bang his baton off his hand, the seated one looking up at the woman for the first time, and recognising her.

"What did you say?" he asked softly.

"I've checked and she isn't. But the daughters of other mothers are there. And sons, too. You should act upon it. Why don't you?"

The standing officer spoke. "What are you, lady, some kind of red?" He was banging his baton off his hand again, this time with more force.

"Maybe," the seated one said softly, "she's one of the gang we've been looking for. Maybe one of those terrorists who make it impossible for decent people to sleep quietly in their beds at night."

"A bomber, perhaps," the standing officer put in. "Ever heard of the Black Death, lady?"

"A fourteenth-century plague," the woman replied, puzzled to be asked.

Both officers laughed sardonically.

The woman continued, "I'm just an ordinary, decent citizen. I simply object to the corruption of the young in this way. Maybe you are not aware of it, officer, but he gives them drugs."

The first officer paused, then spoke again, very softly, "You should be careful of accusing Mr El Blanco. He's a highly respected member of the community."

"You should be very careful," whispered the other officer (bang bang went the baton). "This very night he's sponsoring a charity concert."

"He's a very highly respected member of the community."

The woman refused to be intimidated.

"I saw it with my own eyes," she persisted. "He abducted a child. He gave her drugs."

"Let's say," the seated officer said softly, so softly, "to give you the benefit of the doubt, that the evidence of one's own eyes can be deceptive. You didn't," he went on, "go there alone. Not there."

"You wouldn't have dared." Bang Bang Bang Bang

"You wouldn't have known where to go. A decent person like yourself."

"A respectable citizen."

"Someone took you."

"Some red."

"Told you what was happening."

"Told you what to think."

"And you believed him."

"In your innocence."

"In which we strongly want to believe."

"For your sake."

"For your sake."

"Mr El Blanco loves children."

"He has founded an orphanage."

"He loves those children like his own."

"If he had any."

"He can't do enough for them."

"Honoured citizens like Mr El Blanco have to be protested from the slanders of the envious."

"Mr El Blanco can reply on the protection of the forces of law and order."

"What did you say your friend's name was?"

"No friend of yours."

The woman looked from one to the other in disgust.

"So that's how it is," she said. "He was right, after all."

The seated officer bent a kindly look upon her. "Tell us for your own sake."

The woman spoke with dignity, "For my own sake I'll tell you nothing."

She walked away slowly and with dignity. These monsters wouldn't make her run, though her rage mingled with terror. As she walked away, the seated officer nodded significantly to the standing officer. Fixing his baton to a chain at his waist, removing his cap and putting on a nondescript raincoat that completely covered his uniform, the standing officer followed after her. The seated officer, now alone, stared into space for a moment. This time there had been no tears. He liked them defiant. In the dark, yes, in the dark, she would certainly do.

A necessary evil

At least they had removed the body. In this heat, it was most unsavoury to share a cell with a corpse, however beautiful. Between bouts of puzzlement at being there at all, the amateur artist dozed sitting propped against the cell wall in almost complete darkness now. The only light came through a tiny grating at ceiling level that let out on to the street beside the police station. Too small to consider escaping through, it nonetheless let in a constant runnel of filthy water when it was raining, a torrent when the snows melted, although the amateur artist was not to know this, it being the first time in a blameless life that she had even been near a prison. Nothing now but dust and scraps of burnt paper from a bonfire that was dying drifted down on the prone bodies of the prisoners.

A harsh band of light cut across the cell as the door was opened. The amateur artist's name was uttered in harsher tones by a policewoman, the first woman officer she had seen since entering custody. At first relieved, it took the amateur artist only few seconds to realise that she was after all better off in the hands of the male cops, who were probably reminded by her of their mothers and aunts. She looked like a mother or an aunt. People often told her that, even though she was neither. The policewoman, skinny and muscular and unsentimental, seized the amateur artist's arm in a pincer grip and, although the amateur artist would have been most willing to leave the terrible cell voluntarily to go to whatever fate, dragged her out roughly.

They went to another cell, this time an empty room, brightly lit, windowless. The amateur artist might have flinched if she had known this was one of the notorious basement interrogation rooms, but the policewoman didn't enlighten her. She merely told her to take her clothes off. The amateur artist was no coward, but the sight of the pinched face discouraged her from asking why or refusing. As she was not a prude, either, she simply took off all her clothing and laid it in a neat heap. It crossed her mind that she was about to be raped but in that case, she reasoned logically, why a woman police officer. The woman police officer could, she supposed, be a lesbian, but at the moment, tearing roughly at the amateur artist's clothes, feeling and prodding them, she certainly did not appear to be motivated by lust. And in any case, the amateur artist conceded to herself, looking down at her homely middle-aged figure, there were surely many more attractive women prisoners than herself.

The policewoman seemed satisfied with her search of the clothes, even though she had paid particular attention to the wired brassiere and old fashioned corset that the amateur artist still wore, unfashionably, to control to a degree her bulging flesh. Inside the brassiere, on the left side, over the heart, the policewoman had of course found the sketch of the dead prisoner who looked like Jesus. She looked at it and chuckled, a horrible sound.

The next few moments were among the worst the amateur artist had even experienced in her up to now relatively sheltered life. The policewoman, donning thin plastic gloves, gave her a rough and thorough body search. Though not a prude, the amateur artist found it both a humiliating and painful experience and at last was forced to gasp out, "Why?"

The policewoman looked at her sardonically, "Put your clothes on. I'm taking you to the chief."

The amateur artist was determined not to break. She remembered how the man they called "chief" had entered the cell, how he had kicked the poor dead prisoner who looked like Jesus, how he had shaken and kicked the poor dead body, on and on, endlessly, and then how he had kicked the other prisoners in the cell. How he had kicked her. For the first time, she felt like sobbing, but the sight of the thin pinched face stopped her. The policewoman, she believed, would like nothing better. The amateur artist, slightly bohemian as befitted her calling, but not too much, had always considered the police a necessary evil. Now she was not so sure.

"Comb your hair," the policewoman snapped at her. "I can't take you to the chief looking like that."

"I have no comb," the amateur artist said humbly enough. How could she have, when they had taken everything away from her.

The policewoman sniffed and took her into a small and clean washroom. She allowed the amateur artist to pee – leaving the lavatory door open, of course, but it was better than the bucket in the cell. The amateur artist found speckles of blood on her underpants.

"The bitch!" she thought to herself with unusual venom.

She was allowed wash and a greasy comb was found so that she could tidy her hair — she had been rather alarmed in fact by the wild face that had stared back at her out of the mirror. Then she was led by the same pincers, though this time not quite so roughly, up the stairs, up and up, to the Police Commissioner's office. Had she known he never interrogated in his own room she might have been comforted. Instead of which she suddenly, hopelessly wanted to go to the lavatory again.

A useful haul

The full-breasted woman protester had removed the mask and helmet from the dead pig and had placed them on top of his neatly folded uniform. She glanced without interest at the dead pig's grey and stubbled face, now mask-like in its imperturbability, and wrapped his body in an old blanket. She had made a brief and curt phone call that even the most rigorous tap could not have read as anything suspicious, and then had showered briskly to remove all traces of the pig from her body while she waited. She douched herself but realised she would have to ask Finn for a morning-after pill, to be on the safe side, the cop having ejaculated when she shot him. As she showered, she thought hard. Luckily, during the whole business, the child had not woken up. That would have been most inconvenient. The child, indeed, once an invaluable prop, had become something of a nuisance. It would have been simpler, once they had released her from prison, to have dumped the child where she had found her. The thought has crossed her mind, in fact, but in retrospect it was lucky she had decided against it. She had not known at the time, of course, that the pig was tracking her, but his suspicions would certainly have been aroused if she had left the child in the square and gone home alone.

There was a soft knock at her door. Naked and dripping as she was she went to check it out. It was Finn. She let him in. If he was disconcerted by a wet and naked woman and a dead pig with a hole the size of a baby's fist in his chest, he didn't show it. She explained about the child.

"What are you going to do with her?" Finn asked.

"Take her back where I got her. She didn't wake up. She saw nothing."

"Can you be sure?"

The woman protester started to get dressed.

"Yes," she said.

Neither of them was sentimental. If the child had to be shut up, then so be it. But neither was sadistic either and both were glad it would not come to that. The woman, now decently, anonymously dressed, scooped up the still sleeping child in her arms.

He did not say to her "Be careful" because she always was. She was a cool operator. To kill a pig like that she had to be.

A little later she returned without the child. The masked and helmeted policeman had been wrong even about that. Her maternal-seeming breasts had never suckled a child but only once in a while a compadre whose taste lay that way. No child had ever sprung from her loins. She was always careful. Now she told Finn she would need a morning-after pill and without comment he agreed to procure one for her.

The child she had lain tenderly in a dark corner of the square, asking a woman nearby to keep an eye on her while she went in search of milk. The woman, half-asleep in any case, would not recognise her again. She had covered her head with a black scarf, she had disguised her voice, it was dark. She felt she owed the child she had abducted at least that much.

The body of the pig was heavy and stinking. Between the two of them it was impossible to shift it. They decided to leave it there and move the woman protester out. There was a certain risk in this. Though she had not been there long, some of the neighbours knew her and could describe her. Sure, they were drunks and druggies but between them they could put together an identifiable picture.

"But no one, we may presume," said Finn, "knew he was here. This pig certainly wasn't making an official call. Not with his pants down. With any luck, he won't be discovered before the fires start. And when the fires start, this house will be among the first."

So they left, almost empty-handed, the woman leaving everything, having nothing to carry except the gun, which, carefully wiped, was then dropped on to a heap of garbage in the basement of a dark alleyway where four teenagers were sinking into ever deeper comas and where, behind a much bolted doorway, an almost toothless old crone rocked herself for comfort, clutching her dead cat Francis.

In a plastic shopping bag, Finn carried the neatly folded uniform, the boots and gauntlet, mask and helmet, the gun and the baton of the dead pig. A very useful haul, indeed.

In the abandoned room of the woman protester, the once masked and helmeted policeman was left only with his socks and his stink, which was gradually to grow stronger and stronger, invading the neighbouring rooms, the rest of the house, and finally even arousing the drunks and druggies.

The Connasewer

The Commissioner was munching a doughnut, which left a sugary rim round his lips. On his desk, the amateur artist noticed, as well as a plate heaped with more doughnuts, were scraps of some of her sketches of the square. The policewoman removed the picture of the dead prisoner who looked like Jesus from her breast pocket and placed it on the desk with a salute. The Commissioner looked at it.

"Thank you," he said to her, his mouth full. "You may go."

The policewoman saluted again and left, smiling to herself. The fat sow was for it now, she thought with satisfaction, wondering nonetheless why she had been ordered to bring her to the office, of all places.

"You did these?" the Commissioner indicated the scraps of sketches of the square. One was part of a bright sunlight scene of flower and fruit sellers. It made the Commissioner feel almost nostalgic.

"Yes, they're mine," the amateur artist stammered, "sir."

The Commissioned leaned back in his seat and smiled fatly.

"They're quite good," he enunciated. "Speaking as an art lover and connasewer, dear lady, let me tell you they are really quite good."

"Thank you, sir," the amateur artist replied. The Commissioner didn't look like an art lover to her, but who could tell.

"And this," he smoothed out the picture of the dead prisoner who looked like Jesus, crumpled into the breast pocket of the policewoman and still warm from its proximity to her cold heart. "You did this?"

"I was struck by his face," the amateur artist explained uneasily. "I don't know who he is... was... He was just one of the people in my cell."

The Commissioner frowned. "You were with them," he stated. "You also were with him."

"Oh no," the amateur artist replied honestly but still feeling like Peter. "I just happened to be there. In the square." Then hastily, in case the Commissioner should think she was criticising his officers, "I mean, it probably looked as if I was with them but I wasn't. I was just sketching. Funny time to do it, I suppose, in the dark. But it was rather – well — exciting. The bonfires, the street lights. You know, artistically speaking."

The Commissioner, as an art lover and connasewer, nodded sagely and took another doughnut. After a second's thought, he pushed the plate towards the amateur artist, who unaccountably — she was far too young — reminded him of his auntie. He was gratified to see her accept one with pleasure and eat with appetite. She even left a rim of sugar round her mouth and unconcernedly licked her fingers and wiped her hands on her skirt. In that instant, he decided she was certainly innocent.

"It's a good likeness," he said of the picture of the dead prisoner who looked like Jesus.

"I was rather pleased with it." The amateur artist hoped for her own reasons the Commissioner would give it back to her, but he held on to it.

"You hid it in your brassiere," he commented, his eyes automatically flashing to her ample breasts for a second. Here was one woman, at any rate, who wasn't totally obsessed with streamlining her figure.

"Only," the amateur artist was at least learning rapidly how to lie convincingly, "so the other prisoners wouldn't get hold of it. God knows what purpose they might have used it for had they managed to get it out."

The Commissioner nodded again. The old bird might not look much but she wasn't stupid. He took the unprecedented step of offering her another doughnut. This she accepted without a pause and dispatched as speedily as the first, though by now she was very thirsty.

"You can do portraits, then," the Commissioner stated, at last coming to the point.

"Well, I... Views have always been my forte. That is to say," her mouth was full, "views are what I usually do."

"You see, I was thinking of having my portrait painted. For my wife. As a birthday present." Well, she had given him that horrible framed photograph of herself for his birthday, hadn't she? Tit for tat. He suddenly noticed the gob of spit still veiling his wife's face.

The amateur artist considered. She would have to agree, of course. Could she, should she, use her agreement as a bargaining counter, to ensure her freedom?

"You can stay here until it's done, for convenience sake," the Commissioner pre-empted her. "Then I think there'll be no need to press further charges."

The amateur artist could, of course, have mentioned lawyers and wrongful arrest and false imprisonment but she prudently decided not to. She could have been whisked back down into those dark and sealed cells before you could say knife, those cells in which so many fates had been finally and secretly resolved.

"Stay where exactly?" she asked.

"Upstairs," he replied.

There was a small bright room at the very top of the building, on the roof in fact, the function of which was unknown, although it was occasionally used by police officers wishing to sunbathe, whose natural modesty prevented them stripping off in front of their colleagues. There the amateur artist was to be ensconced, comfortably enough, though as effectively imprisoned as if she were still in a cell. She was to have certain privileges, however, one of which she insisted on, that she not be guarded by the policewoman who had body-searched her. A rookie who could have been her son was assigned that duty instead. First, however, she was required to do some preliminary sketches of the Commissioner.

"You will appreciate," he told her. "That I am an excessively busy man. I can't be posing all day and all night. I hope you'll be able to do a certain amount from memory."

The amateur artist assured him that with the help of sketches, she would only need him for the final touches, if even then. So she sketched. She had a rapid facility which enabled her to dash off five or six studies, all of them giving the Commissioner an undeniably porcine look, crouching over his plate of doughnuts, snuffling into the telephone, even standing to attention, his fat hand on his bloated heart. The last look she thought most appropriate for the kind of portrait he had in mind and so, escorted by the young policeman carrying the canvasses, easels, paints, oil and turpentine he had been sent out to acquire, she ascended to her rooftop room. Once left alone, she spent a long time gazing out of the windows at the near and distant bonfires and musing on the mutability of fate. Outside, on the hard stairs, alternately standing or sitting, the young policeman with nothing to look at wondered at the sufferings that had to be endured for art.

Martyrdom

The new concert hall stood monolithic in the centre of the city between the square and the cathedral. Several acres of semi-slum housing had been cleared — the erstwhile residents sent to the high-rise flats on the outskirts near the fairground — to make way for the new building and for the ornamental gardens surrounding it, not so much gardens as an enormously extended patio with buckets of flowers set on coloured paving slabs, evergreens growing out of concrete, modernistic fountains illuminated in the endless night with changing colours, giant metal sculptures like denuded abstract trees, an open-air bar with waiters dressed as French fishermen, a huge aquarium set in the wall so that the excessively rich patrons could watch exotic fish sashaying through tinted water, while the patrons themselves drank their excessively expensive cocktails, giggling over names like "Stab in the Back", "Gang Bang", "Snuff Movie", "The Phantom of Liberty". And now in honour of the occasion, the proprietor, Anselm, had developed a new drink, "The Martyrdom of St Sebastian." Blood red and ice-cold, but spiked with venom and an excessively high alcohol content, it was proving a wow.

Across the patio, but still visible and audible from the bar, was a large aviary of tropical birds, parakeets, cockatoos. Their harsh twittering evoked thrillingly the jungle, the rain forest, an uncharted, uncivilised, barbaric world.

Everyone but everyone was going to the concert that night. If you weren't going, you were nobody. Everyone who was anyone was enjoying a drink in the open-air bar before drifting in to the concert. The Commissioner's wife was there with her party — unfortunately, as she kept explaining, a huge pressure of work meant that the Commissioner himself would only arrive at the very last minute. She fluttered the bits of mink she had stuck on her eyelashes and wondered where the hell the bastard had got to. Among the Commissioner's wife's party was a small, withered alderman and his large, fruity wife, overladen with jewels as usual, although missing her customary diamond ear pendants, her ruby necklace and her gold charm bracelet. The Commissioner's wife would have given her husband's right arm to learn — for scandalmongering was yet another of her hobbies, perhaps even her favourite — that these priceless pieces were even now adorning the delicate frame of a bearded lady. The alderman looked miserable, as usual. He had tried — the Commissioner's wife could hardly know it — to arouse his voluptuous spouse earlier in the evening by licking her white shoulders. She had pushed him off and told him not to be disgusting, but not before he had tasted the bitterness on her skin, the saliva of the limbless man that still covered her. She hadn't even washed it off. She was still sticky from her encounter. No wonder the alderman looked miserable as he sipped his Martyrdom — and how bitter it was.

His partner, unconscious of her husband's emotional state, was thinking how extraordinary the

Commissioner's wife was looking. Her hair, unaccountably purple, was standing on end as though she had just received a nasty shock, and for some reason she was covered in bits of sticking plaster. Had she cut herself shaving? Should she discreetly inform her, the alderman's wife was wondering, that when she bent over as now, the front of the low-cut magenta dress billowed open to reveal a glimpse of gnarled nipple. Or was that

deliberate? The alderman's spouse squeezed her own heavy breasts with satisfaction. She had never wanted to be skinny. Too many men had told her how much they liked her the way she was. Her plump thighs stuck together in the heat. She wore no tights or panties, and when under the table she opened her legs wide, the sudden rush of cool air felt like a caress.

Inspiration

The piper, preoccupied as he was, had an inspired thought.

"Does your daughter like rock music?" he asked the woman.

"Why?"

"Well, she might be trying to get into the concert. Everyone's going."

"What concert?"

Once again the piper thought to himself that this woman knew nothing.

"The charity concert. The benefit for the orphanage. The social event of the season."

She looked blank.

"The Martyrdom of St Sebastian," the piper persisted.

The woman looked at him as if he were mad.

"It's a rock band. Local boys made good. They have quite a cult following among the young, and older people like it to be thought that they are in on it, too."

"A rock band?"

"Goths."

"Oh no, she wouldn't go for that sort of thing at all."

The piper asked, "How well do you know her?"

"Well enough to know that," the woman answered sharply.

"It's just," the piper went on, "that you're always telling me of things that she wouldn't do. But nothing of what she enjoys. I can't somehow picture her."

(The mirror, the mirror. That fractured face)

"She's just a normal, fun-loving child."

That was surely it.

But the piper wouldn't let it go.

"Are you certain? I mean, children run away from home all the time because their parents don't understand them."

"She didn't run away." The very thought! The woman's eyes filled with tears. "She didn't run away. Something has happened to her."

"All right, all right. I'm sorry. It was just a thought."

The piper was getting tired of all this. Why was he bothering? He had worries of his own.

The woman was staring at her hands. Ropy veins stood out on the backs of them. Her life blood pumping through them. She turned them and looked at her wrists, white where the backs of her hands were brown. Delicate blue branches carrying her life blood to her fingertips.

"All right," she said.

"What?"

"Maybe she likes rock music. Maybe I don't know everything about her after all. Maybe she ran away to go to the concert."

"We'll try," the piper said, "to get in."

They walked across the square, past a child sleeping on the pavement. Really, the woman thought, everything has gone to the dogs. Past the bar, open for business as always, although the singer was elsewhere. Past the heap of bones that was all that was left now of the dead tourist — apart from a wondering memory far distant in the mind of a grey and dowdy woman twisting a gold band round and round a bony finger. Past shadowy figures in corners conducting obscure business transactions. Past a heap of rags that, had the woman examined them more closely, would have turned out to be another sleeping girl-child, abandoned to the elements. Past a mother wheeling a pram endlessly, round and round the square that otherwise was almost deserted. Out of the square towards the monolith that was the new concert hall.

And behind them, from a dark recess, slipped a figure wearing, unseasonably, a dark raincoat. A man with his hands in his pockets, ambling along casually, going wherever the woman went, a shadow without a sun.

A bag of bones

They had brought an old tramp into the police station. He was wearing a jacket with a bloodstained rip across the back that had been identified as belonging to the dead tourist. Although he denied any connection with the murder and although no weapon had been found, the Commissioner was sure the crime could be fastened on to this derelict. Very conveniently of course. They would be pleased it had been solved so quickly and uncontroversially. For a few awkward hours, the Commissioner had been worried that the job might be the work of one of Mr El Blanco's minions. And that would never have done.

"You'd better bring the body in," the Commissioner ordered cheerfully. He might even be able to enjoy his night out now.

But though the two delegated officers went out with a stretcher, they soon realised that a plastic rubbish bag would have been a more appropriate receptacle for the pile of sticky bones that was all that remained of the dead tourist. By the time they reported back to the Commissioner for further orders, they found that he had departed belatedly to ablute and adorn his person, with the help of the valet handpicked by his wife, for the endless night of pleasure ahead. So they went back across the square and wrapped the bones in a stiff starched tablecloth from one of the bar tables. Then they ceremoniously placed the bundle on top of the stretcher and marched back across the square with a hardly heavier load, and carried the lot down to the mortuary. The attendant, however, stood upon his rights and refused to accept something that could by no means be described as a body, without proper documentation. At a loss, the officers wandered around the building for a while, still carrying the stretcher and its grisly load, before deciding by mutual consent to leave it in the Police Commissioner's office — on his desk, in fact — still wrapped in the laundered lawn tablecloth from the bar across the square.

Sold out

The buzz around the concert hall was rising in volume as the piper, the woman and the officer shadowing them arrived. The concert was sold out but touts sidled up to people who looked as though they might not have tickets and muttered cajolingly in their ears.

"Is there any point going in?" the woman asked the piper, looking at the thousands converging on the hall. "Shall we just stay here and watch the people?"

"As you like," the piper replied. He had no wish to have his mind blown by the deafening discords that were the trade mark of The Martyrdom of St Sebastian, so he sat on the edge of a fountain of rising red glass rods and played a tune on his pipe so quietly that few could hear it above the hubbub. But the birds in the aviary heard it and fell silent. The alderman on his way to the concert with his wife heard it as she leaned on his arm. It reminded him for some reason of the mountains and lakes of his childhood, which had been hardly idyllic but which now seemed that way. A large tear trickled, unnoticed thank God, down his wrinkled cheek. He tossed a coin, which fell at the piper's feet. The piper placed a sandal-clad foot over the coin without pausing in his tune. The singer heard it at a distance away as she arrived with Mr El Blanco in his limousine, he as usual all in white and she now all in black, a dress that looked as if it were made from a rough black crepe bandage roughly wrapped around her beautiful figure and imperfectly covering it in strange places, leaving gaps where flesh was visible: under her left breast, over her right buttock. Her hair was piled on top of her head but everywhere was falling in delicate wisps. She smoked an aromatic black cigarette from a silver holder, and her heavy eyes looked far into the distance, through the crowd that stared at her with almost hostile curiosity — the mobster's doll, the gangster's moll. But she listened distantly to the pipe getting louder until she could hear nothing else, it rang in her head, it filled her head as she passed the piper on her silver heels, not looking at him.

"They say," the Commissioner's wife whispered to the innocent little bride of an ambitious young businessman, "they say," she whispered bitchily, indicating El Blanco and the singer, "she dries his feet with her hair. They say he eats his dinner off her naked belly. They say they do everything but... you know..."

The Commissioner's wife was gratified to see the little bride's eyes pop out and thought the effect was worth the slight risk.

"Don't say I told you," she smiled, baring long yellow teeth. It would depend, she thought, on just how ambitious the little bride was on her husband's account. Not enough to be dangerous, she reckoned. Maybe she'd tell her some more things before the night was out, just for the pure pleasure of seeing those baby blues jump from their inexpertly made-up sockets.

Suddenly the woman seized the piper's arm, breaking his tune.

"Let's go in," she said.

He was taken aback at the change.

"Why?"

"I'm curious."

"OK. If you can afford the price of the tickets. This," he tossed the alderman's coin into the air and was surprised to see that it was gold, the price of a memory, "is all I have in the world."

The woman approached a tout.

"How much?"

The tout scanning the crowd for possible customers hadn't reckoned on this dowdy piece. Weren't she and the piper as good as beggars?

"A hundred," he said. "Each."

The woman got out the purse she carried round her neck, inside her blouse.

"Wait a minute. That's crazy," the piper said. "Robbery with violence."

"It's for charity," the tout laughed unpleasantly.

"Give him a hundred for two," the piper told her. "That's more than enough."

The woman hesitated.

"You want to go in, missus," the tout said. "A hundred. Each."

"I'll give you… a hundred and fifty."

The piper sighed.

"Done, said the tout and grinned as he made off with the scraps of paper money.

The woman rushed to the entrance, the piper barely able to keep up with her. Behind them, with a groan, the disguised police officer showed his badge and entered. If there was one thing he hated, it was rock music.

Trick of the eye

Inside, the foyer was a *trompe-l'oeil* of mirrors, high mirrors running up beside gilded staircases covered in gold carpeting. Unrelentingly modern as the exterior of the concert hall was, the interior was baroque, with heavy glittering chandeliers, their sparkling lights reflected infinitely. The long darkness outside had unprepared the patrons for this visual blast. They were dazzled; bright gold specks danced before their eyes. The mirrors confused them and more than one person bumped into his own reflection and excused himself to himself, particularly if he had strongly partaken of Anselm's new cocktail.

The woman held tightly on to the piper's hand as they were jostled on all sides. Truly everyone was here. The moneyed, of course, the emaciated middle-aged women, the fat ones in their designer gowns, vivid silks swathed across wide bottoms, young girls in bright frills, all with the air of somehow being merely the accessories of the dark-suited and powerful men they accompanied. There were the social fliers, public relations and advertising types, graphic designers, media celebrities, the men like peacocks, the women like tropical flowers, tanned, laughing, eyes shooting in all directions to see who was there, with whom, and what they were wearing. Then there were the sullen rock fans in black leather or black cotton, undifferentiated by sex, heavy-booted, long-haired, short-haired, hairless, painted and tattooed, their bodies pierced in strange places. There were sellers of tee shirts embellished with the designs from Martyrdom's new album: **BLACK SUN**, sellers of head-bands and scarves, of compact discs, cassettes and vinyl records, sellers of badges and medallions, and, under the would-be baroque staircases and in the marble lavatories, shadowy figures selling… what indeed? There were the curious, people who just came to look at other people, there were plain clothes police who sedulously avoided catching each other's eye or the eye of the officer following the piper and the woman; there were lads with flagons of drink, though drink was prohibited except as sold at an enormous mark-up from the bars on all floors. There were hairy protesters, their posters folded away for once, music lovers. There was even the old woman in the ill-fitting ginger wig, who waved cheerily at the piper's reflection as she ascended another staircase, arm in arm with her next husband, perhaps. No doubt she recognised the piper from her last husband's chocolate-and-banana coloured hounds-tooth jacket.

Not all

Not everyone was there, of course. The Commissioner was still being polished by his handpicked valet to the degree of perfection required by his wife. The Commissioner couldn't have cared less if he didn't arrive until the interval. He preferred Souza anyway: a rousing brass band.

The tramp was festering quietly along with other prisoners in a dark deep cell. He wasn't quite sure where he was, but this place was like so many he'd been in before that he wasn't unduly concerned. If only he could be sure that the man next to him wasn't dead.

The amateur artist had stopped staring at the endless night and had seized her brushes. It occurred to her that if she could work fast enough, she might be out by morning. Assuming this was, in fact, night. They had taken her watch and she had no idea of the time.

Outside her room, sitting on the stairs, the rookie dozed and dreamed of the farm where he had been reared. It was an honour for the family that he had been accepted as a police trainee and taken to the city, but his dreams were still of the gentle cows he had hand-milked as a boy, the soft rain in the grey light of dawn as he trudged through sticky mud, the smell of freshly fallen rain on earth.

The old crone still clutched her dead Francis, but she too had fallen asleep. Her dreams were more troubled. Someone was sticking sharp points all over her and saying, "Yes, you'll do very well as a pin-cushion." She could hear herself moaning very loudly, thunderously. Or was it, she woke up with a jerk, someone moaning under her window? In dismay, she threw Francis from her, stiff as a board now. Someone was certainly moaning under her window.

She wrapped her arms around herself and started rocking her body to try and find comfort.

Moonshine

Over the other side of town, on the outskirts, on a derelict piece of ground covered with craters and fragments of concrete, the fairground folk settled down after all their customers had dispersed. One or two had even spent a month's pickings and gone to the concert. In the orange tent, the bearded lady curled round the limbless man, on a heap of kimonos. The bearded lady was still wearing the ruby necklace round her waist and the charm bracelet round her ankle, but nothing else. The limbless man stared at the pale orange glow coming through the roof of the tent. He listened to the soft breathing of his companion and smoked cigarette after cigarette, spitting each butt far out of his mouth as he finished it. In the blue tent, an elderly lady midget was ministering to Snow White, who lay as still as ever. The elderly lady midget tenderly pulled a dark blue cover up as far as Snow White's neck, then kissed her on the forehead, before curling up on the floor at the foot of the bed.

The dwarves, Mishka and Rodolpho, and the ugly midget were getting drunk on moonshine as most nights. Rodolpho actually played well on the mandolin, especially when he had consumed a few drinks, and the other two sang in unbelievably sweet voices, the sound flying up into the endless dark, and carried on a slow, slow wind across the infinite plain.

It's so hot

Back at the concert hall, the ticket holders had all taken their seats. The singer in her box, next to Mr El Blanco, and surrounded by the dark and shadowy figures of his bodyguards, looked around the auditorium slowly, with her heavy eyes. At last she caught a glimpse of silver, where the piper's jacket had fallen open across his chest. She sighed so deeply that the reflecting glasses of El Blanco turned to her questioningly.

"It's so hot," she said in her throaty voice, running long fingers over her swaddled breasts as though wishing to rip the bandages off.

It was indeed hot, had paradoxically been growing hotter since the sun disappeared. For some reason, the air conditioning in the concert hall was not working properly. The alderman's wife was running with sweat.

Her silk gown was drenched and clung to her. The unmistakable bitter scent of the limbless man rose from her skin like a miasma and reached the nostrils of the alderman, sitting the other side of the Commissioner's wife. He had only come to the damn concert to be able to sit for two hours next to his own wife. Now he was stuck between this dry stick and the little spouselet of some up-and-coming brat of a businessman.

The Commissioner's wife noticed only that the alderman's wife was sweating pungently and that the alderman was fidgeting a lot. She would have liked to sit next to the businessman's little bride and whisper shocking things in her ear, to make her eyes pop out again. But that could wait. She smiled, charmingly as she thought, like a death's head, the alderman thought. And why was she wearing so many bits of plaster? Had she some horrible disease? He fidgeted away from her.

The businessman's little bride was feeling uncomfortable. She ought to make conversation but she had no idea what to say. Her husband was talking earnestly to a colleague on the other side of her. He hadn't even introduced her. She turned with determination to the alderman.

"It's very hot," she said.

He looked at her abstractedly. He seemed to be sniffing.

"Yes," he said. "It is."

Twinkle twinkle little star

The woman was staring at El Blanco's box. An idea was germinating in her head. Behind her, almost breathing down her neck, was the officer in the raincoat who had been commissioned to follow her. She had a very slim neck. The officer was thinking that he could span it with one of his great paws. He was also thinking that it was a pretty neck, a sexy neck, even. The woman's thin hair was cropped short. She was not the sort of woman he would normally have had dealings with as a woman — too grey and dowdy. But the back of her neck was undoubtedly sexy, the way it was half-turned. He looked in the same direction and saw first a beautiful heavy-eyed face apparently staring right down at him. And then, beyond the face, the familiar bulky outline that was El Blanco. The officer realised with a shock that the woman was staring fixedly at the Boss. Another figure joined the group in the box. The Commissioner, ready just in time, thanks to the valet's efficient ministrations, was paying his respects, even kissing the hand of that half-dressed slut, that hophead, the so-called singer the Boss was always dragging round after him.

The officer looked again at the neck of the woman in front of him. He had to fight off an almost manic urge to run his finger down the side of it. And he was hot, so hot, in his uniform concealed by the raincoat he dared not take off.

The Commissioner, his duty done, joined his wife and her party. The ambitious young businessman stood up to let him have his seat and the Commissioner wedged himself down beside the businessman's terrified little bride. The Commissioner shook hands across her face down the line and then smiled paternally at her.

"And who might you be?" he asked. He liked pretty, fresh-faced young girls. They cheered him up. And he was in a good mood to start with, as no one had yet told him about the dead tourist's bones.

She identified herself timidly. The Commissioner roared with laughter as if she had made a joke and patted her on the knee. Then he offered her some buttered popcorn.

Suddenly the house lights dimmed. On to the stage ran a sparkling figure in an emerald green costume, tight as a snakeskin: the compere, a well-known personality. His high and sugary voice rang out with surprising command and the audience fell silent.

"Welcome, welcome, welcome! Welcome ladies and gentlemen and those in between, welcome to this star-studded megashow, the show of the century. Nay," and now he peeped flirtatiously over his shoulder, "of all centuries past and future, if any future there be. Who cares anyway," his skinny arms shot into the air. "Begone dull care! For tomorrow we rot. You are here to enjoy yourselves, aren't you, ladies and gentlemen. I know the in between ones are, don't ask me how, I just know. Well, you are, aren't you?"

There were sporadic cries of "yes".

"Louder," the fey compere called. "Louder, I can't hear you."

"Yeeesss!" came back in roar from the auditorium.

"One more time."

Virtually the entire audience screamed back, "Yes, Yes, Yeeeeesssss!"

Only the woman stared motionless at Mr El Blanco, who was gazing who knew where out of his reflecting glasses. Only the singer drew on her black cigarette in its silver holder and gazed down at the piper, who in turn was looking down in despair. Only the officer detailed to follow the woman and the piper was staring at the woman's neck and imagining how, if he drew a blade ever so lightly down it, so lightly that she might not even feel it if the blade were sharp enough, bright red beads of blood would bubble up. He had performed this experiment only recently on the body of a prisoner in interrogation room D, criss-crossing the prisoner's entire torso with deeper and lighter cuts and sharper and blunter blades to find how light he could go with an extremely sharp blade and still have the same effect. Unfortunately, the experiment was cut short, so to speak, when the prisoner died of shock.

The alderman was not screaming either, although everyone around him was. The Commissioner's wife looked quite wild, her whole body trembling and the concert had not even started. His own wife was shouting cheerfully. On his other side the businessman's little bride was screaming and giggling as the Commissioner tickled her. The businessman, for his part, was pleased to see her pleasing the right people for once instead of behaving like a terrified mouse. Perhaps she would do, after all.

"Of course you are," the fey compere called. "No need to shout. I'm not deaf. But you're right. Life's short enough, the devil only knows. Party while you can. Dance the night away for there's no tomorrow. There's no tomorrow and that's a fact. And for those in the know, my place after the show. That's a poem, isn't it? I'm a poet and I don't know it. Heard that one before, madam? For those in the know, my place after the show. That's what's called a rhyming couplet, get it? Get it, beautiful biceps? Yes, you in the front row. I mean you. You can come too. We can rhyme in couplets together. Just follow my star..." The compere paused, his painted eyes half-closed, as if listening. Suddenly he opened his eyes wide, and those near enough to notice saw as if for the first time and with a shudder, that his eyes were totally black, as though the pupils had eaten up everything else.

"Well, folks," he chuckled, "It's almost the time you've been waiting for. Almost but not quite. You'll have to put up with me a little longer, yours oh so truly."

There were some good-humoured boos from the audience. The compere fell on his knees, "How I love to be loved! Yes, folks," whizzing to his feet again: the man was certainly lithe, "yours oh so truly Robin Goodfellow, aka Luke Lucifer, but known to my friends as Puck. No darling," amid laughter, "Puck. With a Pee. Puck, your compere for the night. But much more than a compere. Look upon me, if you will, as your fellow traveller on this small part of your journey through the vale of tears. Think about it folks, think hard… Right. Have you thought? Right. You can stop thinking now. That's enough philosophy to last anyone's lifetime. Now for some fun. F.U.N. That's a word that really does start with an eff, darling."

For some reason the Commissioner's wife, along with quite a few other members of the audience were by now weeping with laughter, her yellow eyes almost red. The Commissioner's wife had even gripped the alderman's shoulder and was wiping her made-up face along his expensive jacket, leaving traces of mask and mascara. The alderman tried to catch his wife's eye but she was hee-hawing with the rest.

"Have you heard the one," the compere was continuing inexorably, "about the cannaibal who came back from his holiday with only one leg? He went self-catering."

Delighted boos rang out. How they loved him. If only they'd thought to bring tomatoes they could have thrown them: splat, splat, splat.

"Don't like it? Please yourselves, darlings. Well, what about this then? What's green and red and whizzes round and round? That's right. A frog in a blender." There were more resounding boos. "All right, all right. I didn't write them. And if you don't like them, there are plenty more where they came from. That's right, darling, out of the ark. Just time for one more. Yes? No? No? Yes?"

The Nos filled the hall.

"OK, then by popular demand. Knock, knock."

"Who's there?" virtually the entire audience shouted resignedly.

"Lettuce."

"Lettuce who?"

"Lettuce now listen to that great band, the band you've all come to hear. Yes, folks, it's The Martyrdom of St Sebastian. Yeah!!!"

Ear-splitting cheers and applause carried Puck offstage where he fell into the arms of his personal assistant, a large and filthy gypsy, who carried him off bodily to a dressing room with a small but twinkling star on the door.

Pinned down

An ancient cathedral stood in the centre of the city, a focus of pilgrimage, a magnet for visitors. It had been, in fact, high on the agenda of the dead tourist before death itself carried him beyond souvenirs, postcards and photographic snaps. It stood a looming darkness during the day but was oddly salient at night when it was floodlit by a score of powerful lamps. Now, in the endless darkness it was the only place in the city outside of the concert hall to go to be dazzled, its grey stone turned blue-white by the bright lamps. But no one apparently wanted to be dazzled, no one was near. Even the beggars that in daylight lurked in the shadowy recesses of its buttresses and porticoes, had now disappeared into cosier subterranean holes.

This endless night the cathedral was empty. The priests, monks and nuns had all gone to bed or, in the exceptional case of Brother Joachim, to the rock concert in drag. Brother Joachim, who was no longer young, looked, to tell the truth, rather homely in a pink nylon blouse and pleated navy blue skirt with sensible shoes. Nonetheless, someone tried to buy him a drink and he was half-sure the compere had winked at him from the stage. And why not? Hadn't Brother Joachim taught the little runt geography not so very long ago, when his name was neither Robin Goodfellow nor Luke Lucifer either, but something far more prosaic, which the Brother, whose brain was too full of the names of mountains, lakes and cities to retain the distinguishing tags of boys, had completely forgotten.

So the ancient cathedral stood empty in the middle of the dark city, blazing like an ice-cold fire from the time when someone had thought to turn the lights on. Blazing like a beacon across the almost infinite plain.

Inside, nothing moved. The soaring vaults seemed to hold down rather than release. They seemed, by the glow of the flickering candles and the bright blue-white of the flood-lights outside that poured coldly through the stained glass and left blood-red and acid green and petrol blue and sulphur yellow streaks on the stone floors, to be pinning down the impulse to soar. Only the flickering candlelight on the faces of the bland saints, pastel virgins and angels, only the glow of flickering candles seemed to cause these holy ones to frown for a moment. This wasn't right, this emptiness, this hollowness. Where were the devout? Where were the prayers that should rise like incense into the highest vaults? Where were the crashing chords of the organ that should fill the cathedral to the roof, almost breaking out into eternal space, only that the stiff stone managed always to hold it back, pin it down? Where was all this? Where? And where, above all, was God?

Crackling

It was dawn. No doubt about it. The old crone had not dared even to hope until she was sure, but now there could be no doubt. Rosy fingers were scratching at the sky. The nightmare would soon be over. The unthinkable could remain unthought. Soon she could go out.

Nearby, in the blazing building, the skin of the dead riot policeman was slowly turning into crackling, yellow smoke pouring from his pungent body. In vain, the drunks and druggies that inhabited the building tried to summon help. The fire brigade was out attending to some of the other numerous fires that had suddenly and at once sprung up over the whole city, whether by spontaneous combustion engendered by the intense and growing heat, whether by the sinister intervention of shadowy figures with cans of petrol, the fire brigade had no time to ponder. And of course all the bosses were at the rock concert.

Just like that

The Martyrdom of St Sebastian completely bowled over its fans. No amount of listening to recordings, the *cognoscenti* agreed, could compare with a live performance. The Commissioner's wife, who considered herself *au courant* with the younger generation — and was she, after all, so old? — felt icy fingers run up and down her back. She screamed and tore at her hair, at her skin, like the youngest groupie. If only the band hadn't absolutely turned down the invitation to attend or even put in the briefest appearance at her soirée. Of course, it was the fault of the band's manager, the slick bastard. The band itself had probably not even heard of the invitation, had probably not even been given the choice. That slick bastard! No doubt, he considered the Commissioner of Police not prestigious enough. The wrong image, no doubt. A prior engagement, he had told her slimily: the Boss had already invited them. The "Boss" indeed. She might have known, even without her husband telling her, even without her husband's valet telling her. The "Boss"! Still screaming in apparent ecstasy, the Commissioner's wife peered with glinting eyes through magenta claws at the box where the big man in white sat impassive behind his reflecting sunglasses, where his mot sat carelessly staring away from the stage as if this wasn't the greatest social event since the visit of the Pope (another one who had oh so politely refused the Commissioner's wife's invitation to a *soirée*). The bitch could hardly keep those hooded eyes of hers open. She was on something for sure. The Commissioner's wife wondered if all the tales were true. She hadn't told that pop-eyed little bride a fraction of it. Suddenly she saw a woman enter the box behind the Boss. Suddenly restrained by the Boss's bodyguards. The Commissioner's wife grew tense with excitement. Some insignificant woman, some dowdy woman in grey had walked into the Boss's box. Just like that. The woman was shouting and screaming — the Commissioner's wife could tell by the way her mouth was opening, by the way her face was contracting. Only no one could hear it, not even apparently El Blanco himself, because the music of the band drowned out everything, even itself. The Boss's bodyguards manhandled the woman out of the box, the door of the box was shut and no one but she, the Commissioner's wife, had noticed anything. That was a satisfaction of a sort, that was pleasure. The Commissioner's wife squirmed in her seat, her skirt rose to the top of her bony thighs, she tore at her face, drawing blood, and screamed and screamed and screamed.

Lost daughters

It was quite a long time before the piper noticed that the woman was no longer at his side. He had been preoccupied. He had been formulating an elaborate and crazy plan. Now he had no idea how long she had been gone. When, after three endless numbers, she still failed to return, he went in search of her. It was with relief that he left the auditorium. God knew he wasn't there for the clash of discords that tore at his senses and left them shredded.

The singer had seen the woman leave her seat. She had seen, although she had pretended not to notice — pretending not to notice being a pre-requisite of those near the Boss — how that same woman had forced herself into the Boss's own box and ranted on and on about some lost daughter. The singer couldn't understand why the woman was making such a fuss. She had lost daughters herself too, probably. And sons. She was almost sure that she had. She closed heavy eyes. When she opened them again, the piper had already left his seat. A silver trail, like a snail's, marked his passage. The singer's heavy eyes traced the silver trail out of the hall. She touched the flesh of her breast below the black bandage and held her breath. Without a focus for her, the squirming writhing multicoloured mass below her had no form and she felt dizzy, as if about to plunge into chaos.

Tonite!!!

On stage, The Martyrdom of St Sebastian was reaching a climax. The lead singer, clad in tiny strips of studded black leather that bit into his flesh like bonds, threw his sweat-gilded body into ever greater convulsions, paroxysms of death or sexual abandon. Women in the audience opened damp legs, men's penises grew harder. Behind the lead singer advanced a row of musicians wielding instruments like weapons, death's heads on their tee-shirts. They sang of pain and destruction and black death and everyone heard but few were listening to the message. *Tonite!!! Tonite!!! The fires are already burning. the bombs are in position. The hairline cracks will widen into jagged chasms. Tonite!!! Tonite!!! The blood is already flowing. It will flow in rivers. Tonite!!! Tonite!!! I have my gun, baby. My gun is cocked, baby. Put my gun in your cunt, baby. I'll blow your mind.*

The Commissioner's wife, whom the Commissioner had never managed in twenty-three years of marriage to bring to orgasm, ululated with so many others in uncontrollable frenzy.

Lucky

The woman was lying on the patio outside the Concert Hall, where the minions of El Blanco had dumped her, unconscious but no more hurt than necessary. The minions knew better than to rough anyone up too much at the social event of the year, a charity function moreover, where El Blanco was presenting his squeakily-cleanest aspect. Sunk in the shadows of the concrete pillars was the officer following her. He had lurked outside the box, unable to believe it when the woman just walked in on the Boss. He had lurked until the minions had dragged her out, gently for them, though one held his great paw over the woman's mouth to stop her shouting. He had tiptoed down the would-be baroque staircase after them and had seen them push her out through the great glass doors with just enough force to ensure that she would not come back in again. The officer didn't feel sorry for the woman. He reckoned he was lucky to have got off so lightly. She could have landed him in deep shit if he had been spotted. The Boss would have judged that he should have kept her clear of him, particularly on this evening of all others. The officer for his part couldn't understand why the piper fellow hadn't tried to stop her. The guy certainly had enough cop-on to know the risks run by anyone trying to get too close to the Boss. But the piper had seemed to be asleep. Asleep! In all that racket! The officer's own ears were still ringing. He wouldn't be surprised to find he was permanently deafened. When the woman had got up and left her seat, the officer had nearly given the piper a helpful nudge. Get after her, friend. See what she's up to. Only of course that would have blown his cover. He stared sourly at the woman, still unconscious on the patio. Never mind her neck, he'd like to slit her throat. And how easy it would be.

Then the piper emerged and picked her up like she weighed nothing. The guy just picked her up. He had to be stronger than he looked. He just picked her up and carried her in his arms. The officer hoped they would now go home, wherever home was. He himself wanted to be tucked up in bed beside his plump wife more than anything in the world. The piper, carrying the woman, turned back, however, turned back towards the square.

Falling fruit

The woman was lying on the ground. It was hard and grey. She was so hot. So hot she could hardly breathe. Looking round her, above her, she saw the enclosing glass of the conservatory. The door was locked. She couldn't get out. They had locked her in. Was it possible? Was it possible they could have been so cruel? If she could have lifted herself up ever so slightly, she would have been able to see the rose garden beyond the glass of the conservatory. The rose garden now at its peak of perfection, buds and blooms perfectly rounded, moving slightly in the gentle breeze that wafted their perfume right up to the glass of the conservatory. But not through it. Oh no. It was impenetrable. Her nostrils were filled with the rotting smell of a tropical forest. She could hear the birds singing. Splat Splat Splat as one heavy, over-ripe fruit after another fell on the hard grey floor, all around her, falling, rotting. But she couldn't get up. Her body wouldn't obey her. Her arms and legs were as heavy as marble blocks. Splat. A fruit fell right by her head and broke open, running red with pulp and juice. Splat. She opened her mouth to scream but no sound came out.

If she could have lifted herself up, she would have been able to glimpse the rose garden. She might have seen them then in the rose garden, laughing and walking. She might have seen him breaking off the heads of roses for the girl. She might have heard the girl's cruel laughter as she tore the petals from the perfect heads,

strewed them on the ground and danced them into the path.

   She felt herself lifted up. The piper blew a soft breeze over her from his open mouth. He was whispering soft words she could not hear. She could not hear his words because the birds were cackling, whistling and laughing so loudly. The piper lifted her up as though she weighed nothing at all. He lifted her and carried her away from that terrible place into a dark tunnel that closed comfortingly about her.

Warts and all

It was not only the singer who had been watching the piper. The old woman with the ginger wig had been keeping an eye on him, too. It was difficult not to notice him in the last husband's eye-catching chocolate-and-banana checked hound's-tooth jacket, in which nevertheless the piper looked very well. The old woman felt she had reached an age when it was incumbent on her to find a young husband. The elderly crock who had escorted her to the concert, the crock of eighty with his pendulous wart was really a last resort.

The old woman in the crooked ginger wig didn't know what was the relationship between the piper and the woman but she felt that it couldn't be close. Not after what had happened between the piper and herself at the seedy café while the woman was sleeping. The old woman looked at her arthritic hands with their enlarged joints, at her vermilion fingernails. She examined her hands and found faint traces of silver still lodged in the wrinkled folds. A young husband would be nice. A penniless young husband above all, who would owe everything to her. Very nice indeed. So it was with pain and regret that she saw the piper leave his seat in the theatre to follow the woman. And when, much later, she touched the elderly crock with the pendulous wart and her hands sank deep into his cadaverous flesh, she was left bereft and for the first time in her long life, afraid.

Lemon sherbet

The ambitious young businessman was delighted with his evening. He had been seen and noticed. His bride, whom he had married in a moment of aberration — what in heaven's name could she contribute to his career? — had after all not let him down. Certainly not, even if her eye make-up was applied somewhat inexpertly. Perhaps that very lack of expertise, which often irritated him so much, was in fact what made her charming to these world-weary sophisticates. For his little bride had been seen with the wife of the Commissioner of Police, no less, who, it was already being said, had taken her up. The colleague sitting next to him had actually remarked, possibly with some envy — his own wife being a dog — "I see the Commissioner's wife has taken up your little lady." Not to mention the Commissioner himself, who was obviously smitten with her. For himself, although the noise made it impossible to hold anything like a normal conversation, he was gleaning a lot from the colleague sitting next to him, a lot of dirt he could use when necessary.

The young businessman's little bride, had he but known it but he never would, was altogether less happy. The Commissioner, for one thing, kept tickling her and while at first it had genuinely made her laugh, by now it was hurting and she was merely pretending to enjoy herself. On the other side was no respite. The alderman was constantly sniffing and saying nothing. As for the band and the music, she herself preferred something more melodious and less ear-splitting. A nice young man with a guitar, for instance, like the one who had played and sang at her cousin's wedding. What a nice young man he had been, she thought hysterically, as the Commissioner's paw found her ribs again, those songs of the wandering life and of the woman who gave up her feather bed and her rich husband to follow the raggle-taggle-gypsy-O, and all the time the nice young man playing the guitar had been looking at her, she knew it. She peeped reluctantly at the pornographic gyrations of St Sebastian — surely the thing was blasphemous, but no one, least of all the Commissioner's wife, seemed shocked. Suddenly, the Commissioner inserted his hand under her skirt and although she was protected by pantyhose and cami-knickers, she froze into immobility. For the sake of her husband's career, she would endure all but take no pleasure in it. The Commissioner for his part, sat back somewhat soothed. He needed soothing for he had finished all his snacks, his buttered popcorn, his three packets of crunchies, even his liquorice toffees. But this was better than sucking your thumb and almost as good as a bag of lemon sherbets.

Lust

The alderman was deaf, dumb and blind. He was filled with the bitter scent of the limbless man rising from his wife. Surely everyone in the hall must be aware of it. Maybe it was the source of the strange intoxication that had overtaken, for example, the Commissioner's wife on his right, squirming, screaming and writhing, and the businessman's little bride on his left, frozen stiff. His own wife, as he could see from the corner of his eye, was sprawled in the attitude of lust momentarily satisfied, lust ready at any moment to be reawakened. Her soaking wet dress hung to every luscious curve. She was, mouth half-open, sucking her thumb, a strange gesture in a woman of middle age. Had the alderman known it — and best for his peace of mind that he should not — his wife was having a fantasy in which she tugged the limbless man around with her on a little trolley, like a pet mutt on a leash. She was seeing herself at banquets, a symphony concerts, at rock concerts, at society dos, in a long wide skirt with nothing on underneath. She saw herself having tedious conversations, with tedious mayors and tedious wives of mayors, with porcine Commissioners and their yellow-eyed bitches, with this luminary and that jumped up nonentity, and all the while her pet mutt was rearing up unseen under her skirts between her wide apart legs, servicing her as only he knew how. She smiled at the thought and caught the eye of her useless husband. He thought she had smiled at him — such a smile of sensuous anticipation, he groaned in despair, until the frozen little bride of the businessman felt constrained to melt enough to yell at him through the noise to find out was anything the matter.

Mud and bones

For once the amateur artist just could not get it right. Whatever she did, the Commissioner turned out looking like a pig. Rejected canvasses lay scattered round the little room at the top of the building like illustrations to Animal Farm. And then there was the background. While she had done some rapid sketches of the Commissioner himself, she had failed to take note of the details of his office.

She did not possess either a photographic memory or the capacity to create a suitable background out of nothing. She was simply an amateur artist who could do a passable copy of whatever she happened to be in front of, whether inanimate or animate, the only exception so far being the Commissioner himself.

She decided to leave for a time the lineaments of her subject. If she could only revisit his office, she was sure that getting the background right would inevitably encourage her to recreate authentically the aura of the man himself. But she knew she would never be allowed to do such a thing, not while the Commissioner himself was absent. No harm in asking, nevertheless. She knocked timidly on the door of her room. No response. She knocked again. Nothing. Had her guard gone? She tried the door, locked of course. She peered through the keyhole and saw the key in the lock on the other side. The amateur artist slid a sheet of paper under the door and then, with the end of a small paintbrush, pushed the key gently out of the lock. It landed with a jingle on the sheet of paper. The amateur artist pulled the sheet back under the door, with the key on it. Nothing could have been easier. She opened the door and, carrying her easel, her paints and her canvasses, she left the bright little room at the top of the building.

Outside on the landing lay the rookie, fast asleep, his mouth open. He was dreaming of brown fields sticky with mud. He dreamt that he lay in the mud naked, laughing, rolling in the sticky mud that smelt peaty, the rich scent of ancient forests. He was thirsty. If only he could get to the stream at the bottom of the field. Delirious with pleasure, dying of thirst, he rolled down the field, his whole body brown with peaty mud, down towards the stream whose waters he could already hear babbling over rocks, the stream of dark brown water that would taste like wine.

The amateur artist crept by him. Maybe, she was thinking, if he woke and saw her, he would shoot her, believing she was trying to escape. Nevertheless, she paused to look at him. His face was beautiful in repose, almost as beautiful as the face of the protester who looked like Jesus. But the face of the protester who looked like Jesus had lines of suffering carved on it that made it to her eyes even more beautiful. This rookie's face was that of a child, open and innocent, still awaiting the sculptor's knife.

The amateur artist went down the stairs making, despite her bulk, no sound but the rustling of her skirt that could have been the wind in the reeds by a stream in a field. The real danger would come when she reached the lower flights, for surely there would be more people around, more officials, perhaps even the stringy policewoman who had subjected her to that degrading search. The amateur artist felt sure that if she happened upon the policewoman, the woman would have no compunction whatsoever about putting a bullet into her. Still, she had to finish the Commissioner's portrait. She had agreed. It was a point of honour. Even if he had kicked the body of the dead protester, the protester had been dead by then and had felt nothing. Even if he had kicked her in the cell. Subsequently he had behaved honourably towards her — hadn't he even given her two of his doughnuts? Hadn't he acknowledged her skill as an artist? — so that naturally she had to complete her commission.

Here was his office. She recognised the padded door. It would, of course, be locked and the whole endeavour would be a wasted effort. It was unlocked. Then someone was in it. She opened it and entered. No one was in it. She shut the padded door behind her and bolted it. The amateur artist looked round in pleasure. An opulent room that would reproduce well. She set up her canvas in front of the desk. On the desk was what looked like a rolled tablecloth. Lying under the tablecloth and beside it were her own fragments of sketches, the sketch from her bosom of the protester who looked like Jesus. The amateur artist pulled it out from under the tablecloth, noticing a faint stain upon it. She pressed the picture to her lips and then replaced it inside her brassiere, close to her heart. There was more than one matter of honour to hand.

She examined the tablecloth. It was in her way. When she lifted it up, it felt heavy. There were stains on it. She opened it out. The bones, picked almost clean, lay in a strange configuration. The amateur artist was no wise woman but perhaps such had been among her ancestors, for she felt a stirring in her beyond horror. There was no skull — the head of the dead tourist had rolled unnoticed under a bar table where it still lay — but she recognised the remains as human. She touched them lightly and blood stuck to her fingers. Dazed, she returned to her canvas and began painting as never before.

Where's Winkowicz?

Back at the Commissioner's multimillion mansion – *chez nous*, as the Commissioner's wife liked to call it — preparations were in train for the *soirée*. In the great kitchen, laid out in rows, the ingredients of each dish: *crevettes* with black grapes, quail soup *aux cerises*; two swans — one black, one white — stuffed with oysters; calf cooked in its mother's milk; skewered eels; brain salad garnished with pickled walnuts; green figs in syrup, lark pie, lambs' tongues in aspic, mares' milk cheese fricassed in vine leaves. And dozens of velvety red flower heads were heaped in baskets, ready to be deep fried at the last moment: diabolical roses.

Because of death threats against the Commissioner — an occupational hazard — masked and helmeted police constantly patrolled the grounds. Each day, one was even delegated to the house, though ordered to keep an inconspicuous profile since the Commissioner's wife complained that he clashed with the decor. She had wanted, in fact, to have the duty officer dressed in full Samurai armour, but for once the Commissioner held out, aided by the unanswerable argument that, weighed down with the unfamiliar armour, the officer would be seriously impeded if called upon to fulfil any life-saving duties.

Still with a powder of golden pollen on her hair from the sunshiny morning — now an obscured memory — and from the bouquet of orange and yellow, crimson and gold flowers whose damp fresh scent she even now recalled with delight and longing, although it had long since faded from the spiked heads of the blooms in the Commissioner's wife's arrangement, the languid maid suddenly came upon the cop guarding the house in deep and serious conversation with the Commissioner's personal and handpicked valet: that same valet, so smiling always, so friendly, so eager to hear all your secrets, confidant of the master and of the mistress, too, and of half the household if it came to that. Well, she for one didn't trust him, his sparkling brown eyes, his ready smile, his efficient brown hands, so nimble-fingered he could unbutton the Commissioner's tightest waistcoat in a trice. And now how pleased she was to think that she had never told him anything. Not her: she was too cute. Whispering in a corner with cops! She might have known. It stood to reason. She ran thin fingers languidly through her thick hair and a shower of golden pollen fell around her. A snitch! She would have to keep an eye on him.

The masked and helmeted cop finished his most interesting chat with the valet and lumbered off. How heavy the uniform was, like a Samurai's armour, how unlike his customary light and stretchy gear, how difficult to get used to moving freely in it. How hot it was and what an overpoweringly pungent smell arose from it.

"Hi, Mirandolo!" one of the other cops had said to him, recognising the smell. He had grunted back, which wasn't strange because that was all Mirandolo ever did. And what if the roster said that Winkowicz was the house duty officer for the evening? What of it? So Winkowicz had swapped with Mirandolo. Nothing strange about that, it happened all the time. Everything was normal, everything in order. The other cop had moved off to start his constant patrol of the grounds without a second thought.

What wasn't normal, however, was that Winkowicz wasn't off on a date. He wasn't getting laid for free by a beautiful whore in return for overlooking some possession charge. He wasn't screwing some poor bitch of a frightened housewife who had been caught shop-lifting trying to feed her five children after her husband had as usual blued all the money on booze. He wasn't even visiting his own wife in hospital nor going to his father's funeral. Winkowicz had none of the official and unofficial excuses to account for his absence. In fact, strictly speaking Winkowicz wasn't absent at all. When the Commissioner's personal and private valet went to the Commissioner's dressing-room to hang up the Commissioner's ordinary everyday uniform alongside all the other more elaborate ones — the military outfits of three decades hanging stiffly on their hangers like a parade of the rulers of a minor military dictatorship — he would find, if he cared to look, Winkowicz lying stiffly behind the uniforms, a stiletto in his chest from which a small trickle of blood had spread in a rather artistic pattern, what had been Winkowicz now resembling nothing so much as the plate of trout in raspberry coulis at that very moment being prepared down in the kitchen. Winkowicz even shared with the trout the same glazed and slightly affronted expression on his face.

The valet didn't care to look. He rather disliked corpses, even while admitting that they were at times an unavoidable necessity. In any case, where could Winkowicz have gone? Only the valet and the Commissioner possessed keys to the dressing-room and the Commissioner had long gone to the concert. The valet skipped off to attend to other duties, taking care to lock both the dressing-room and the bedroom doors behind him, and taking special care to hang the keys on a chain around his neck. He smiled a sparkling smile at the languid maid with gold dust on her dark hair, who was lounging in the corridor doing nothing in particular. The valet felt the key to the locked dressing-room burn cold against his breast. He was looking forward to the evening ahead, even though he realised that it might, after all, be his last.

The languid maid, who was keeping an eye on the valet, while dusting in a perfunctory manner the not exactly Ming vases in the corridor, was on the other hand not at all looking forward to the evening ahead (not realising it might be her last). No, indeed. It would be work, work, work. It would be watching those gluttons permit themselves every sensuous luxury, degrading themselves once more in front of their servants and not caring because they didn't regard their servants as being of any importance. It would be seeing the avid yellow eye of the Commissioner's wife, in the middle of an animated conversation with some old duffer, follow every move the servants made in order to find an excuse to ridicule them in front of the guests, and later to cut a few shillings off their pay.

The languorous maid smelt the flower she had abstracted from the Commissioner's wife's bouquet, the flower she had hidden in her bosom. Its sweetness still evoked distant fields, morning dew, sunshine.

One of her duties was to spray the Commissioner's wife's flower arrangement with perfume. She would do it now, get it over with. If she used enough, the scent would linger until the arrival of the guests. She chose a carafe of the Commissioner's wife's most expensive, least floral perfume, and descended the stairs to the dining room, banqueting hall, as it pleased the Commissioner's wife to call it (the trough, as the languid maid thought of it). The arrangement stood in the middle of the long French polished mahogany table. In the heat, the exceptional heat for the time of year, the flower heads were already wilting. The maid sprayed them with water. There was nothing more she could do for them. Their gorgeous petals were already writhing in the agony of their death throes. The languid maid's eye was caught by a splash of black, the congealed blood from the Commissioner's wife's finger spotting the petals like the clue to a recent assassination. She emptied half the carafe of expensive perfume all over the spiked flower heads and fled. The handpicked valet caught her in the hall.

"Go home," he said. "This is no place for you. Go home to your parents' house in the country."

The bastard knew everything, even without being told. Even about that house she had left forever in order to see the world.

"Go home," he said, his bright brown eyes glittering. "Go home now."

The languid maid tossed her black hair, showering the valet with golden pollen. So that was it: he wanted her gone. Laughing harshly, she went into the kitchen and shut the door on his anxious face.

Sleep

Water splashed over her, cool water that made channels in the dust on her face, water that spotted the grey of her dress with black.

"Let me take you home," the piper was saying tenderly. She was almost seduced. "Let me take you home."

He could carry her so easily down the dark tunnels of streets, back back to the spidery house. The door would open easily — why should it not? There were no keys now. He could carry her into the dark house and up the stairs. He could lay her tenderly on the narrow bed and cover her with cobwebs. At last she could rest.

She reached out to put her arms round his neck and then remembered.

"No," she said. Her face was mirrored waveringly in the moving waters of the fountain. Her face. And the other one?

"No," she said. He gave up. Mostly he gave up easily. He was not the pushy sort. He felt for the soothing comfort of his tin whistle. Later he would play it.

"I have to go now," he told her. "I have something of my own to do." He had figured it all out so clearly.

"You'll come back?" she asked him.

"Yes," he promised, though not firmly. Who knew?

He could have taken her to his shelter. It wasn't far. She could at least have slept undisturbed. She needed so much to sleep. But he had other plans. He ran a finger tenderly down one side of her withered face.

"Yes," he promised more firmly. But who knew?

The piper walked away, passing a mother pushing a pram, her steps regular, her eyes fixed ahead of her. The baby slept quietly and soon the woman did too, while, sweating and restless, the officer consigned to follow her waited in the shadows, the pinpoint of red fire from his cigarette the only sign of his presence.

Mountain climbing

Sitting in the stalls, wedged between women not his wife, the alderman was thinking of the mountains of his childhood. They stood ranged above the small town where he had been reared, stood higher and less accessible than the mountains over the city where bonfires still gleamed. It was almost impossible to imagine that small town now, tucked in the valley between those mountains where he had played as a boy, looking up with longing at the high pass that wound between them to somewhere even more enticing. He saw in his mind the open slopes dotted with bright yellow and blue flowers, the occasional tree blown sideways in the constant wind, the tumbling waterfall over green mossed rocks. He saw the boy that he had once been struggling up the slope on and on and up and up, searching for the top of the mountain that always seemed to be over the next rise and the next and the next, till suddenly he was almost precipitated into a valley with its own fields and farms, on and on. Resting and eating a bun and an apple and then racing back down the slope at breakneck speed. He had always promised himself he would go back. Wasn't there yet time? Wasn't there?

What, he thought, if he had stayed there? Become some pillar of the local community, married some

healthy country girl whose father owned a farm with high pastures. Would there have been five or six progeny of his own now to give him pleasure, instead of this sterility, this impotence? Or was there something in him that would make any woman shrink in horror from bearing his child, as his present wife had done? He began to get agitated again. Then forced himself to think of the mountains, to imagine them as they must be now at this moment, standing splendid and indifferent. It was time to go back, he was thinking. It was nearly time to go back. He had always promised himself that he would return before he died. He sat, a still point in the middle of all the noise and writhing. Everything slipped away from him. He stood on the lower slopes of the mountains, looking up at the high pass that led between them. He stopped sniffing, and the little bride of the ambitious young businessman looked at him for a moment in surprise, aware of a change, until called back to her duties by a particularly intimate tickle from the Commissioner, whose finger had only jerked involuntarily as he slipped off himself into a blissful slumber. Better than sucking your thumb.

This involuntary jerk, however, shocked the businessman's little bride into grabbing the nearest object. To avoid the Commissioner himself, she had been reduced to the alderman, who was still climbing the lower slopes of blue mountains. He blinked. He looked around himself wildly. It was nearly impossible to believe that even at this moment those distant mountains stood silent and cold. A cold that couldn't be imagined. And was he now seeing things? It seemed that the concrete walls of the concert hall were billowing and ballooning out at him. He stared at them. There could be no doubt. A great crack had appeared on one wall. No one else seemed to notice, but why should they when all eyes were focussed on the obscenely cavorting crew on stage.

Hypnotised by the sight, the alderman saw how the billowing walls seemed to be melting and dripping in the heat. Silver metal was trickling down them. Great globs of sticky white liquid pushing its way through the cracks that were opening up everywhere. The alderman tried to catch the attention of the Commissioner's wife, but she was half-lying across her seat, one dried berry of a nipple exposed, her skirt hitched above her thighs. Her eyes were closed and she was sweating, gasps emitting from the gash that was her mouth. The alderman turned to the little bride of the ambitious businessman but she returned his gaze with blind terror, the great paw of the blissfully snoring Commissioner pinning her where she sat. Panic grabbed the alderman by the throat. He clambered over the Commissioner's wife to where his own spouse was sitting oblivious, miles away across the city, in an orange tent. He gripped her arm and tried to pull her out. At first, she pushed him back with irritation but then she too, led by his wild eyes and waving hands, saw the imminent collapse of the building. She started shrieking, but her voice merged with the screams of the audience. He tugged her out, clambering over oblivious fans, pulling her hysteria towards the nearest exit. He pushed her out into the endless night and dragged her over to the fountain of red rods. The alderman and his wife both plunged into the tepid water that hissed in contact with their hot skin. The effluvium of the limbless man, the taste of his saliva, washed off the alderman's wife at last, washed off her into the water of the fountain and rose up the red rods briefly turning them sulphurous yellow. The alderman drank the water of the fountain thirstily and tasted not the thirst-quenching freshness of a mountain spring but the bitter saliva of the limbless man, the flavour of lust and betrayal and corruption. His wife lay limp and exhausted in the tepid water and though he no longer particularly wanted her, the alderman began to copulate with his wife one last time, there in the fountain. He raised his head from her vacant face and saw the mountains loom ahead of him, as he remembered them, as he desired them. He walked up the steep slope, he passed between the walls of rock, clambering higher and higher. In daylight, he could have turned and seen the little town nestling in the valley, but now it was dark and cold and he could see nothing. Up and up, stumbling and blind and panic-stricken. His foot hit a rock, he turned his ankle painfully. Twisted trees formed startling shapes on the skyline. On and on, up and up. Branches tore at his eyes. He reached out to steady himself and his hands met slimy wet rock, slippery rock. He tumbled back. This was not as he had imagined it. He had imagined a refuge, not a trap. He was lost. He recognised nothing in the looming shapes of darker darkness. He didn't know where he was. He would never know where he was.

Why were things never as you remembered them? Why was it impossible to go back and find things unchanged? He should have known. He should have guessed. His wife lay back, gasping and spluttering in the water. He hardly recognised her now. There was no going back. There was no climbing now to the dancing waterfall. The alderman, with great deliberation, crawled through the fountain and wedged his head under the concrete ledge from which the red rods rose. He wedged his head tight in under the waterline, so that when his body tried to make its involuntary fight for life, it was almost instantly defeated. His wild eyes saw the red rods rise wobbly above him through the water: his last glimpse before water flooded his lungs and a black curtain fell upon him. It was not a dignified end but then, in recent times, the alderman had abandoned all dignity.

A thief in the night

Over the other side of the city, Mishska, Rodolpho and the ugly midget were in the last stages of drunkenness. Rodolpho could get no sweet sound out of his mandolin any more, and the other two merely croaked. They finally settled down together under the heavy sky, and dozed and snored and at last fell into the deepest slumber. Nothing woke them. Not the stray dogs that nosed their faces, licked up the spilt liquor and pissed on them. Certainly not the figure who had been waiting, waiting for hours for them to fall silent and who slipped by them at last like a streak of moonlight and as silent; that slipped into a certain tent where a certain person was lying still as death, and came out again soon afterwards carrying a large bundle as if it weighed nothing. Not even the elderly lady midget curled on the floor at the end of a certain bed awoke, so silently did the intruder move. She only dreamed that a moonbeam slid briefly over her face.

Brushing his hair

At the time when a small number of people were starting to make an orderly but rapid exit from the concert hall, other buildings in the city were responding to the heat. In the same way swelling and bubbling and dripping and melting. Only one remained unaffected: the ice-cold cathedral under its harsh blue-white floodlights.

People rushed out of the concert hall in their eagerness to get away, barely noticing the woman lying wantonly in the fountain, not noticing at all the dark shadow wedged under the concrete ledge from which the red rods rose.

El Blanco and the singer were long gone, whisked away in the white limousine. The Commissioner's wife's party had stumbled out depleted, though not yet noticeably, in numbers. Many others stayed. As long as the band played on many in the audience refused to leave. In any case, no actual announcement had been made as surely it would have been if there was any real danger. Some members of the audience, indeed, thought that the billowing and oozing walls were part of the act. Stunning special effects. Laser bright lights cut through the darkness of the hall as the band hammered out encore after frenetic encore.

In fact, no announcement was made because there was no one to make it. Behind the tiny twinkling star on his dressing-room door, the compere had long ago recovered from his exhaustion, aided by the filthy gypsy and a hypodermic syringe. He had changed his outfit from emerald green to clinging crimson, and his black eyes glittered like wet stones under salt waves. As he freshened up his make-up and dusted his eyelids with peacock-blue powder, there came a soft tapping on his door. It was so soft that at first neither the compere nor the filthy gypsy could hear it. Finally, the filthy gypsy opened the door and admitted a boy who looked like an angel, golden-haired, golden-skinned, dressed all in white.

"I'm a present," the boy whispered. "I'm a present from Mr El...."

The compere put an entranced finger to his lips. He glanced at the filthy gypsy, who nodded.

"Wait," Luke Lucifer said. "I'm nearly ready."

He started to brush his long thin hair with a bone-handled brush. Then passed it to the boy.

"You do it," he said.

Very softly, very gently, the boy brushed Luke Lucifer's long thin hair. Then the three of them left the building by the stage door, climbing into the black limousine that would take them to the party. Near the door waited a dowdy middle-aged woman who stepped forward at the sight of Luke Lucifer. The car headlamps shone in her face.

"Brother Joachim or his twin sister," sighed Luke Lucifer with delight. "Will we take him with us. Will we? Will we?"

The filthy gypsy's impassive face broke into a leer.

"Yes," whispered the boy.

The car door was opened and Brother Joachim entered, leaving behind his old life forever.

Murderers

The old crone poked her long nose out of the unbolted door. Her weak eyes saw that the sky was red. It must be day already. She would make her statement. All would be well. She left her little room, catafalque to Francis the cat, and stepped out into the yard.

Suddenly she saw them, huddled in the shadows in the corner, and her timidity left her.

"Murderers!" she screeched, rushing at them.

They stared at her blankly. They had groaned all night and she had not listened. Now they were past all groaning. She peered at them, knowing something was amiss. Her foot hit an object on the ground. Not another dead cat because it was hard and cold. She picked it up. A gun.

"I'm warning you," she said, pointing the gun at the huddled figures. But they neither moved nor winked, just continued to stare at her. In the red, flickering light they were strangely grey, they were cold as marble when she touched their still faces. Now she knew for sure that these were not the murderers of Francis the cat but perhaps the victims of the same murderers. She would avenge them all. Cocking the gun as she had seen it done year by year on television, the old crone advanced up the metal staircase, into the bright and flickering city.

Gone!

"Snow White has gone!" The elderly lady midget shook Mishka roughly, trying to bring him back to consciousness. "Our Snow White has gone!"

The dwarf returned from the edge of the garden of paradise where he had been dancing with a mermaid. He walked through grey fog heavy as water, hearing the shrill voice of the elderly lady midget and seeing her face wobbling in front of him.

"Snow White has gone! Snow White has gone!"

Rodolpho stretched and scratched.

"Gone where?"

"Do you mean woken and gone?" asked Mishka, the mermaid having already swum away forever.

"I don't know. I don't know. She's not there, that's all."

The dwarfs and midgets rushed to the blue tent. The couch was empty, their darling gone. The ugly midget burst into wailing howls.

"Look," said Mishka, pointing to a faint silver trail on the ground, "a slug was here."

The fairground inhabitants rose out of their holes at the sound of the wailing midget. They gathered silently around the empty couch. They stared at the faint silver trail leading out of the tent, over the broken

ground and towards the city where it became lost under pounding feet, under dust and ashes. They stared silently and then, wrapping themselves in blankets, or grabbing coats to cover their nakedness, they set off in a train to find their darling. All of them: Mishka, Rodolpho, dwarfs and midgets, the strong man, the lady contortionist, the bearded lady and even the limbless man, carried over the humps and bumps of the waste land to the road, where he was put on a little trolley with wheels and tugged along by the bearded lady, just as if he were her pet mutt.

Thus it was that when much later a fat and bedraggled middle-aged woman limped into the fairground, she found no one there except the elderly lady midget, left because someone had to stay in case Snow White was returned and because she was, after all, too old and feeble for a prolonged search. The middle-aged, fat and bedraggled woman found the elderly midget weeping beside an empty couch in a blue tent. The middle-aged woman sat down on the floor and wept beside her.

Part of the furniture

The cop they called Mirandolo wanted to kill her but the handpicked valet was against it. Another figure, full-breasted, lolled against the door frame, watching them coolly.

"We can't let anything, anyone, stop us now. We can't afford to run any risks," the cop known as Mirandolo was saying.

"We'll lock her up, knock her out, until afterwards," the valet replied. "She's not one of the guilty ones. She's a victim."

"Precisely. A victim. One of those that falls both ways."

"It doesn't have to be like that."

The handpicked valet looked to where the languid maid was lying in a white slip, stripped of her black uniform, bound and gagged and terrified on his bed.

"I told you," he said gently, "to go home."

"Don't you agree with me?" the cop they called Mirandolo asked the full-breasted woman by the door.

She hesitated. This was no moment for sentiment. On the other hand, the girl could not move, would not go anywhere.

"It might be kinder to kill her now," she said. "Who knows what might happen to her later? On the other hand, she presents no danger to us as she is. She doesn't look much like Houdini to me. I think he's right." She jerked her head at the valet. "She's not one of those who deserves to die."

"OK," said the cop they called Mirandolo. "If you say so."

"The Commissioner's bitch has pots of sleeping pills," the valet said. "We could make her take a good dose of those."

"OK."

The cop they called Mirandolo was not pleased. Still, he was willing to go on with the decision for the time being. He could always, he considered privately, slip back later and tighten the gag a little too much.

"I'll fetch the pills," the valet said. "You get ready."

While he was gone, the full-breasted woman lifted off her own loose dress and dropped it to the floor. Then she picked the maid's uniform off the bed and struggled her way into it.

"Will it do?" she gasped. "I can hardly breathe."

"It's not for long," the cop they called Mirandolo replied doubtfully. "It'll have to."

When he returned with the Commissioner's wife's sleeping pills, the valet, relieved at having saved the maid for a time at least, laughed out loud on seeing the way the full-breasted woman bulged out of the uniform. The buttons were stretched almost to popping across the bosom and the fabric pulled back to reveal white flesh beneath. The skirt, hitched up at the back over her wide buttocks, showed several inches of sturdy white thigh.

"No, no. You're far too eye-catching. The bitch will have a fit. She likes her servants to be part of the furniture, almost invisible. I'll get a larger size from the store-room. I won't be long. You give her," he jerked his head at the maid, "four of these." He passed the woman a bottle of white tablets. "Four's enough. Any more might be dangerous. And you," he turned to the cop they called Mirandolo — but of course Mirandolo himself meanwhile lay cooking like a joint of pork in a blazing building downtown that the fire brigade hadn't even bothered to try and save — "get back on duty or you'll be missed."

He skipped out. The woman glanced at the man in the pungent uniform of Mirandolo.

"You hold her down while I give them to her."

She poured four tablets into her palm and looked at them, gleaming white as pearls. She glanced at the man again and poured out four more. He nodded at her. The woman found a glass and ground the tablets into it. Then she took a flask of brandy from a carrier bag and poured a large slug into the glass. She swished it around so that the grains of the tablets were well distributed throughout the drink. She looked down at the cop. He pinched the maid's nose, slipping down the gag at the same time. At last the maid was forced to open her mouth and the woman emptied the contents of the glass down her throat.

"You'll sleep like a baby now, darling," the woman said gently, as the maid coughed and spluttered. "Now,

now, don't spit it out or I'll have to give you some more."

The man dressed as Mirandolo replaced the gag. He looked at the full-breasted woman.

"I'll see you later," he said. And left.

The woman pulled back her hair. The bruise on the side of her face, inflicted earlier by the masked and helmeted policeman, gleamed livid yellow and blue and purple. The full-breasted woman covered it with make-up from the maid's dressing table. As it was still only incompletely disguised, she let a swathe of hair fall forwards over her cheek. It would have to do. When the valet came back at last with a large black uniform, the full-breasted woman tore off the maid's too tight dress and put on the new large one that engulfed even her. Finally, she took a belt out of the carrier bag and, lifting her skirt, fixed the belt loosely around her waist. The belt held two pistols and a knife, that when in position, dangled under her belly.

The valet meanwhile sat on the bed stroking the hair of the still-whimpering maid, who gazed at him with her terrified brown eyes. Later, when he looked at his hand, it seemed to be covered in gold-dust.

Red dress

No one noticed the wan figure of a ten-year-old girl child clamber down the mountainside, her thin dress illuminated from time to time by the glow from the bonfires, her red dress, once so pretty if rather adult for such a skinny child, now torn and dirty. The worshippers, the sacrificers, huddled, drugged by smoke, round the glowing fires, too far gone to pay attention to the comings and goings of children.

Cess pits and carnivals

Out of the corner of a half-closed eye the woman saw the piper enter the square, gently carrying a heavy bundle. She rose to meet him, as he hastened towards her.

"Have you found her?" the woman enquired anxiously, looking at the bundle. "Have you really found her?"

"Where's your house?" the piper asked urgently.

"What?"

"Can we go to your house, right now? It's very important."

"I'd rather not." the woman recoiled.

The piper fixed obsessively gleaming eyes on her. He lifted a corner of the blanket. The woman peered fearfully at the white face, the abundant auburn hair.

"Snow White!" she sighed. But after all, she should have known. "You're mad."

"I've only borrowed her."

"Do your freaky friends know that?"

"I won't be keeping her long. I'm just... conducting an experiment."

"You've stolen her! You've stolen their star attraction. They'll tear you to pieces if they find you with her."

The piper looked slyly at the woman. "I'll take her back in a minute," he replied.

"Take her back right now."

"What is it to you?"

"Have you abandoned me? What about my search? I want you to show me where El Blanco lives. I want to catch the beast in his lair."

Now the piper looked amazed.

"You mustn't even think of it."

"Show me where he lives."

"I don't know. And even if I did, I certainly wouldn't tell you."

"I only want to ask him a simple question," the woman said. "He can't refuse me. A mother."

The piper looked at her sourly. "I'm afraid he isn't the sentimental sort," he said.

"He can't be bad all through. No one is. He sponsored that charity concert, didn't he. He endowed an orphanage."

The piper jerked his head.

"Can you be that naive? He runs a hostel for the nubile young. You've seen some of the inmates."

"He has, or had, a mother of his own, didn't he? I

can appeal to his better nature, his finer feelings."

At that, the piper threw back his head and laughed. Across the square, the dark and still figure of the watching officer wished he could share the joke.

"Don't judge everyone by your own standards," the woman said coldly.

"What!"

"What are you thinking of doing with her?"

"You have a filthy mind."

"I didn't have before today," the woman said sadly. "Today I have seen such things I never even dreamed of. You showed them to me."

"They were there all the time, only you never looked."

"The whole world is a cess-pit. Is that it? Have I learned my lesson?"

"No," said the piper. "That's the whole point. That's where you, in your single-mindedness, make your big mistake. Yesterday was white. Today is black. But that's not how it is. The world is a carnival of colours, brilliant, clashing and splendid. It's beautiful."

"Now you're contradicting yourself."

"That's all right, too. The world is full of contradictions. Before yesterday, you thought the world was all good..."

Did I, indeed? considered the woman.

"Now you believe it to be all bad. But it's both together. That's the paradox. That's the wonder of it."

The poor fool is in love with a dream, the woman thought.

"You have been very kind to me," she said. "Just do this one last thing. Please."

The piper looked at her.

"I can't."

"You can't be bothered with my problems now you have her. I understand."

"That's not it at all. I still want to help you. I want to help you by not doing what you ask."

The woman looked at him.

"I'll let you hide her in my house. If you tell me where I can find El Blanco."

A frightening sacrifice, after all. On both sides.

"All right," said the piper.

The rookie had been awakened roughly by a boot kicked hard into his side. He opened his eyes and saw the stringy policewoman towering over him.

"She got away," the policewoman was hissing. "You slept and she escaped."

The rookie turned blindly and saw the door of the little room wide open and the room beyond empty.

"And these?" the policewoman inexplicably shook sheets of paper in his face. "What about these?"

The rookie looked at the sheets and couldn't help bursting out laughing. All the sketches were of the Police Commissioner in various poses but each one looking precisely like a pig.

"She's caught him to a T!" he exclaimed.

The stringy policewoman whacked him on the side of his face with a leather gauntlet.

"Well, since you find the whole thing so funny, you can explain it to him yourself," she snarled. "I'm sure the Commissioner will see the joke. How you fell asleep guarding her and let her escape."

The rookie was fully awake now and knew that he was finished.

"Perhaps I can pick her up before he finds out," he muttered.

The stringy policewoman jeered.

"You'd like that, wouldn't you, you little bumpkin. No, you can stay here until the Commissioner comes back. You see, under the circumstances, I don't think I could trust you not to run away."

She pushed the rookie into the room and, brandishing her gun in his face, made him take off his uniform down to his shorts. Then she gathered up his clothes and threw them out of the room.

"Don't try anything, pet," she smiled, her cracked teeth ghastly in the pale light. "I shall be sitting outside." And she cocked the gun and aimed at his testicles. Then she raised the gun and shot out the light bulb. "I have excellent aim." And laughing, she slammed the door, leaving the rookie for some moments in impenetrable darkness. Gradually his eyes grew used to it and he saw the pale line of light under the door, the dull glow from the windows.

He huddled for a while, considering. He was lost, of course. Irretrievably. It was simply a matter of time. His eyes overflowed with tears that ran down his cheeks. So young to be lost. One tear ran down his nose. He licked it and tasted the salt sea. Looking out of the window, away beyond the dark lump of the mountain, across the endless plain, out there, out there was the sea. If he could only reach it, he would be safe.

Paint

Down in the Police Commissioner's office, the amateur artist was painting compulsively. Far away was the sudden sound of a shot. She paused for a second, listening, but there was only silence. She painted on, her hair hanging loose and dishevelled and dappled with colour round her large face, down her wide shoulders. She sweated. Her clothes were drenched and felt clammy against her skin, so she pulled them off, her blood-spattered underwear, too: naked at last, painting all the time. Occasionally she inadvertently smeared herself with ultramarine, with cadmium yellow, with rose madder or viridian. As she worked, she muttered to herself. As she muttered, the bones on the table hopped and shuddered, and away under a distant bar table, long white worms entered and exited through the winking eye sockets of the dead tourist.

Dust

The spidery house was silent and dark. The woman had fled. Shown him the door and fled. Up dusty stairs climbed the piper, gently carrying his bundle. Dust rose at every step. Up and up the stairs. Cobwebs brushed his face. His bare feet sank into soft dust. Ahead he could make out a landing. A mirror on the landing. A door. My darling's door. Oh!

Another little hobby

It was party time. the Commissioner's wife burst gaily through the cordon of police into the mansion, tugging behind her the new favourite, the ambitious businessman's little bride. Behind her, shuffled the Commissioner, looking furtive and eating honey-coated almonds from a bag stuffed into his pocket.

The handpicked valet stepped forward, sparkling, to relieve the Commissioner of his overcoat. He laughed and joked with the Commissioner and winked at the Commissioner's wife. As more and more valued guests arrived, the cop they called Mirandolo, discreetly positioned behind a Corinthian pillar in the hallway, studied their faces and grinned behind his mask. Only two were absent now: the small alderman and his spouse. The Commissioner's wife made an obscene comment which the businessman's little bride didn't understand.

The guests were shown into the reception room, where a full-breasted maid offered them drinks, but the Commissioner's wife did not notice that this was not the usual languid maid, for she had grabbed the valet by one hand and the businessman's little bride by the other, and had darted girlishly (as she imagined) towards the stairs.

"I'm soaking," she laughed. "I just have to change."

The businessman's little bride had been dazzled by the mansion, the hall, the polished staircase. She had never known that people really lived like this. It was like in one of those old-fashioned films. The Commissioner's wife reminded her of one of those old movie actresses, living in a luxurious house with just such a curving marble staircase. The apartment she herself shared with her husband the businessman was expensive but tiny. It had been his bachelor pad before marriage and would do, as he said, until the children started arriving. A prospect that made his little bride shiver with fear.

But this! Like in the films, she thought, like a palace, and she said as much to the Commissioner's wife who smiled, gratified.

"Isn't she perfectly sweet!" she said to the valet.

They reached the Commissioner's wife's room, or boudoir, as she liked to call it. A sensuous place, all purples and blacks and magentas. All velvets and silks and furs, surfaces that called out to be stroked. The handpicked valet lit the black candles on the mantelpiece on either side of a large, gold-framed mirror, and the flames danced in reflection. They danced again in a long mirror on the opposite wall, back again, and so on into infinity. The businessman's little bride had never seen anything like it. When she at last turned, she found to her consternation that the Commissioner's wife had stepped out of her dress, which lay in a puddle on the floor.

"She's never seen the like," the nude Commissioner's wife laughed to the valet, who remained unmoved.

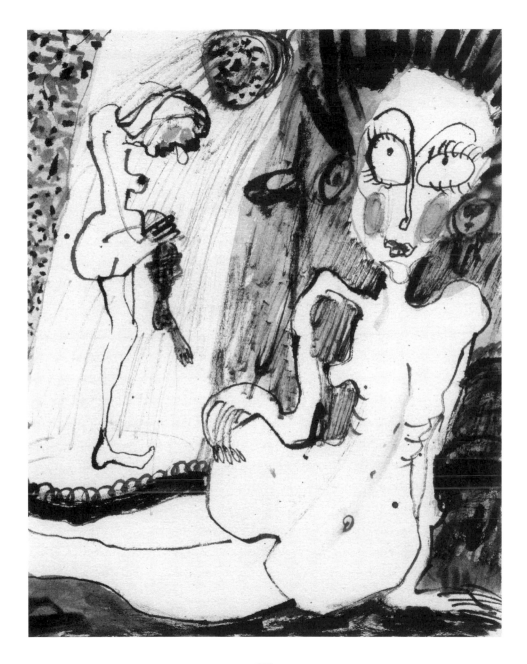

He had seen the like all too often. "Isn't she perfect!"

For the businessman's little bride's pale blue eyes had almost burst from their sockets.

"The lime green, I think," the Commissioner's wife was saying. "But I must be stinking. I'll shower first. Would you like to shower, too, darling girl?"

"No, thank you. I'm all right."

"It would freshen you up, you know. You could borrow a dry dress. I wish you would. I almost feel like insisting."

After the fumblings of the Commissioner, the businessman's little bride felt soiled. A shower would be very welcome. The Commissioner's wife was really very kind. Also, she was thinking, her husband would like her to be agreeable.

"Perhaps..." she said, not noticing the alarmed eyes of the valet.

The Commissioner's wife trilled with joyful laughter.

"Show her where," she ordered.

"After you," the businessman's little bride said politely. The Commissioner's wife laughed all the more.

"Not at all. I'm having a drink first. To cool me down. Take all the time in the world, darling."

The handpicked valet led the businessman's little bride to an en suite shower. His eyes were filled with pity and he handed the girl, against all the rules, a fluffy towel.

Back in the boudoir, he opened the walnut cabinet that concealed the refrigerator, and prepared a drink for the Commissioner's wife, who now lay curled on the purple silk bedspread facing a long wall mirror in which she studied her reflection, smiling softly. She looked, when she smiled, like a crocodile. The valet handed her a tall glass rimmed with salt and thought, pacifist as he was, lover of humanity as he was, how he would enjoy inflicting pain and torture on this terrible woman. But not yet. His eyes sparkled down at her.

"Now for the floor show," she whispered. He crossed to the wall mirror and pressed a button.

Now the glass became transparent and the girlish form of the businessman's little bride could be seen beyond, removing her cami-knickers, her tights. The Commissioner's wife sighed and sipped her drink.

"Perfect," she said.

It was another of her little hobbies.

The girl-child in the torn and soiled red dress walked across the square, past the place where, a moment before, the woman had been talking to the piper. She walked past a mother pushing a pram. A tramp stretched out his hand automatically to her but she had nothing to give him. She walked on firmly, past the bar, pausing by the table. She lifted the starched cloth of the table and peered underneath. The head of the dead tourist wriggled and trembled with new life. He seemed to smile up at her. The girl-child let fall the flap of the cloth and walked on. The cloth crumbled into ashes. She walked past the still sleeping infant appropriated briefly long ago by the full-breasted woman protester. She was about to touch her as she slept, but the sleeper moved and the girl-child did not want to wake her. She walked on, past shadowy figures that barely glanced in her direction, on and on, out the square, down dark and stinking alleyways. She passed a troupe of midgets and dwarfs, a strong man, a bearded lady dragging a limbless man on a little trolley, a lady contortionist. They looked at her with sad eyes but did not speak to her. She walked past the gleaming cathedral and tried its doors in passing, but they were locked. As she passed by, sighing, the doors split in twain.

She walked into a cheap café, where an old woman in a crooked ginger wig sat on the lap of an old crock with a pendulous wart, sinking scarlet taloned fingers into his soft flesh. She walked right up to the counter where mask-faced women flicked soiled boas at her, and, seizing a stale roll, stuffed it into her mouth. It tasted newly baked. She walked out again, circling back, past buildings billowing in the heat, across a patio covered in potted plants, now shrivelled and dead, past Anselm's cocktail bar where young men giggled as they drank "Vagina Wine" and young girls, staring at tropical fish in the aquarium, sipped thick sweet concoctions of white rum and coconut juice: "Nuns' Shrouds".

She walked past hanging cages where birds chirruped mournfully or threw themselves against the bars. She walked over to the bulging and billowing concert hall, now frothing and writhing like an epileptic in a fit. She stretched out her hand and touched the large ugly building — the band had left long before although their music still resonated within and, up until the last minute, holograms mimicked their gyrations and burnt shadows into the concrete. The moment she touched it, the hall gave a great shudder, cracked and imploded, burying forever with it the melted bones of the last remaining fans. The explosion caused the doors of the

cages to fly open and brilliantly plumaged birds to take off over the city, screeching and flying wildly. At the same moment, the aquarium cracked in two, spreading water and tropical fish over the patio pavement. Glasses in the hands of the young men and girls at Anselm's bar splintered into tiny fragments and as the bar itself slipped into an opening abyss in the ground, the young men and girls tore with bleeding hands at paving stones to save themselves.

At the same moment, the red rods of the fountain burst, the pressure of water forcing up the body of the dead alderman, shooting it high into the air, and apparently defying the laws of gravity, for it was not seen to come down again.

The girl-child in the soiled red dress looked in wonder at the devastation apparently wreaked by the touch of her hand. Then she smiled quietly to herself and walked on.

You ain't seen nothing yet

It was party time. A black limousine streaked through the dark streets of the city, past blazing buildings that illuminated for a few seconds the wildly grinning face of Luke Lucifer, the gravely angelic face of the boy, the ravaged face of Brother Joachim, the dirty face of the gypsy driver. The black car flashed through the Street of the Innocents, Luke Lucifer waving gaily at the pimps and prostitutes, out beyond the Street of Innocents and into dark and steaming laneways beyond. The filthy gypsy drove fast through the maze of narrow winding streets. He knew this part of the city like no one else. Brother Joachim, looking out of the rear window of the limousine, caught a brief glimpse of the coldly illuminated cathedral, which stood on the very edge of this pit. Then it was blocked off from his line of vision.

The car stopped abruptly, flinging the passengers forward. They were in front of a high dark building in a block of high dark buildings in a narrow alleyway. The gypsy driver got out and with insulting obsequiousness opened the doors of the car for the passengers to get out.

Luke Lucifer led the way. He had been here before evidently, for he skipped down a flight of metal stairs to a basement door. He knocked cautiously, an elaborate pattern of knocks, and the door swung open.

The party had been going for a while and the maze of basement rooms were already full and noisy. As the compere danced in, people briefly attached themselves to him with light kisses and moved off. The boy followed him gravely and people oohed with delight to see such a beauty. Brother Joachim hesitated, it is true, for a moment, before entering and perhaps only entered at all because he was pushed from behind by the filthy gypsy. Brother Joachim had first been taught to believe in hell and then he had been taught to believe that hell did not exist. Privately he had guessed that hell dwelt in the soft and silky dresses that hung under the heavy scratchy robes in the wardrobes of his cell. The dresses that seemed to him to smell of the woman he often wanted to be. But now he thought that perhaps he was wrong, after all, and that hell was indeed here, in this dimly lit and smoky basement club, where addicts gaped blankly at dark glass panels, seeing who knew what horrors reflected therein, where beautiful young girls and boys gave themselves up openly to the intimate caresses of the terminally diseased. The Empress, the queen of the club, an obese elderly man with grey flesh, heavy grey breasts, simpered in a corner, continuously sipping through a straw at a thick yellow cocktail which, since his own hands shook too much, was held for him by a naked young Negro boy. As soon as he finished one drink, the boy fetched another, the Empress whimpering all the while the boy was gone. A skeletal old man thumped his chest and spat out gobs of phlegm or blood on the floor in front of him. If you paused, he grabbed your arm in his claw and whispered obscenities in your ear. He pulled a shrivelled tube of skin out of his pocket and informed you that it was the penis of his long-dead beloved. Elsewhere a girl-child and a boy-child danced on mirror-topped table, crudely aping adult love-play, while thin women screeched with laughter as the children pulled off each other's clothes and stuck baby fingers into each other's flesh.

Joachim gazed at these and other horrors. Then closed his eyes and tried to pray. When he opened them again, he found Robin Goodfellow hopping in front of him, grinning wildly.

"Pray for us sinners, brother. Pray for us in your padded bra, in your pretty frock. Pray for us. Now and in the hour of our death. Which I'd say, ain't too far off." The compere spun round laughing shrilly. "But sister," he screamed. "You ain't seen nothing yet."

Suddenly, a strobe light was switched on. Joachim saw, as in a film, the weirdly jerking movements of the compere, of the club members who screeched and screamed. The addicts rose from the floor puzzled and afraid, a woman had a fit. Joachim rushed from the room, trying to remember the way he had come in. But wherever he turned there were smoky panels, dead end corridors, locked doors. At last a door opened and he flung himself through. But behind the door, smiling through a mouth of blackened stumps, was the filthy

gypsy, a reel of thin wire in his large hands. And behind the gypsy, giggling like mad, Joachim saw the tiny figure of the compere, whose ears he had boxed, whose knuckles he had rapped, whose buttocks he had whipped so many times in years gone by. The names of all the lakes, cities, rivers and mountains were suddenly blotted from his memory. Now all he could think of was a boy's name. Not Puck. Not Robin Goodfellow. Not Luke Lucifer. A very ordinary and even banal name.

Ready

The old crone limped through flickering streets, the gun held ready. She had nearly fired it off at several indistinct and shadowy forms that had seemed to loom up at her out of dark corners but then had melted away. Her vision was not the best these days. Now smoke and fumes made her eyes sting and water. Tears ran down her cheeks. She had no idea where she was going but followed the lights of the fires towards the brightest fire of all.

The key

The spidery house was not as silent as the piper had thought at first. There were constant whispers and murmurs. Inexplicable draughts caused curtains to sway. A door slammed, boards creaked, a tap drip dripped but the piper could not find where it was, to turn it off. Still, he felt cosy here with his beloved. He felt safe. She lay as beautiful as ever, as still as ever on the bed. He remembered her lightness, her softness, as he carried her. Her neck, under the ear, was soft and warm and he buried his face there. He felt a feather-light pulse beating through her. He pulled a cobwebby blanket over her feet and legs in case she took a chill. He stroked her lovely face. Then he opened the window and stood and gazed out across a dark and rose-scented garden to the city, blazing now in parts, as black as death in others. The flickering fires reflected on low thick clouds, almost as if, he thought, it were dawn. Almost as if the sun were about to rise. The piper took out his pipe and began to play a thin and sad tune. Did she move? Did she? Or was it a ghost that made the cobwebby blanket stir and flutter slightly. The piper played on.

If she would only move, only moan, only wake. The thin and reedy tune fluttered out over the city. The birds released from their cages were attracted by the sound and flew to the window of the room. Some even flew inside and perched noiselessly on the bed. The thin and reedy tune was carried by a light rose-scented breeze far over the city, beyond the bright square where now the dead tourist's head bobbed in time, past the still and gloomy cathedral where saints waited for other music, other scents, past the boudoir where the singer was preparing her beautiful body, turning at the tune and almost remembering, down dark lanes to where a troupe of dwarfs and midgets, a strong man, a bearded lady tugging a limbless man on a trolley, were wandering in search of a silver trail. They lifted their heads and listened. They heard the sad piping and tears rolled down their cheeks. The ugly midget howled a terrible and despairing howl. The piper, in turn, heard the howl and shut the window rapidly, trapping several exotic birds inside. He wondered how he could have been so foolish. He seized his tin whistle and pressed cold, despairing kisses on Snow White's forehead, on her cheeks and wide lips. Thus he left her to the care of the ghosts and shadows and, piping softly to lure the birds after him, he descended the dark and dusty stairs into the shadowy hallway, out the door, closing it gently behind him.

Then he led a false trail over the city, piping all the time, piping down dark alleyways, piping down streets lit brightly by burning buildings, round the city square, up the mountain side, down down into the dark city again, down steaming streets, the Street of Innocents, piping his sad tune. The old crone cocked her gun at him, then smiled at the soothing tune until it faded from her deaf ears. The old woman in the ginger wig heard him pass her bedroom at the moment when she was sinking her talons once more into the eighty-year-old crock with the pendulous wart. She screeched and pushed him from her. The old crock, knowing when he wasn't wanted, put in his teeth, put on his clothes and descended with dignity into the cheap café, where he sat in a corner and waited for death or a cup of tea.

The imprisoned tramp, sober now, and convinced that the man beside him was truly dead, heard the tune waft through the grating of his cell and settle over the filthy puddles on the floor like an epiphany. He put his hand in the half-ripped pocket of the dead tourist's jacket and pulled out a key. The key did not fit the cell door and the tramp nearly threw it away in disgust. Then he remembered that a key always fits some lock or other and decided after all to hold on to it.

The piper piped on. The troupe of midgets and dwarfs heard him. Now near, now far away, but they tramped on and on, after the song, after the sad call.

In the webby house, Snow White slept, not hearing whispers and creaks and low moans, not feeling the lightest touch of a breeze or a ghostly hand on her, not seeing a dim face peer out from a dusty mirror hanging on a wall on a dark landing.

Greed

The Street of Innocents was quieter than usual when the woman stepped uncertainly into it. It was quieter because it was party time and most of the regulars were out partying.

The pimp with a philosophical bent didn't care much for parties so he lolled as usual against the wall, picking at his teeth and waiting for business. He eyed the woman, wondering what her game was.

"Excuse me," she said to him.

"Yes, darling?" he replied. Business wasn't exactly booming and he was ready to be diverted.

She looked at him, as he thought, stupidly.

"What you want then, eh?" the philosopher pimp asked her. "Too shy to put it into words, eh? Let me guess?"

He whispered in her ear, taking the opportunity at the same time to lick it.

The woman jumped.

"Certainly not," she said. "I want my daughter."

"She ain't here." Not another one of those, the pimp thought.

"I know that," the woman continued. "But I was hoping… Maybe Mr El Blanco would help me find her."

"Who?"

"Mr El Blanco."

The pimp spat a gob of green phlegm at her feet.

"Don't know the gent," he said.

"You must know him," the woman persisted. "Mr El Blanco. The top man. The big boss. Comprende?"

The pimp roared with laughter.

"Mr El Blanco, eh? Now who's been filling your little head with stories?"

"This morning I saw him take a child from the square. Later I saw her here with him. He gave her a bonbon. Then you sent her off with an old man."

The pimp looked at the woman with loathing.

"Oh yeah?" he said. "You seen a lot, ain't you, lady. Sharp-eyed, ain't you. Too sharp-eyed for your own good."

"I don't care what goes on here," the woman lied. "All that matters to me is getting my daughter back. I just want to see him. Maybe he knows something. Maybe he can help me. They told me you would be able to show me where to find him."

"They told you wrong, then, didn't they. As I said, I don't know the gent."

"I only want to ask him if he knows anything about my child." The woman drew out a purse from inside her blouse. "He seems to know everything that goes on in this city." She drew a wad of money out of the purse.

"Oh yes, lady?" the pimp said, his eyes flickering over the purse which the woman was replacing inside her blouse and on the wad of money in her hand. Who would have thought it? The old bitch was loaded! "That's true enough." He licked his lips. "Eyes and ears everywhere, he has."

"So will you take me to him? Please."

The pimp backed off.

"Oh no. No, no, no. Not me, darling. I keeps me nose clean. I knows when I'm well off."

The woman peeled off notes from the wad of money and offered them to the pimp.

"Please," she said. "Please."

"My considered advice, lady," the pimp said, taking the whole wad, "would be: forget it. But I see," stuffing the money into a side pocket of his tight green trousers, "that you've made up your mind. Come on then. I'll point you in the right direction."

A furtive rat-faced little man scurried out of a doorway, saluted vaguely at the philosopher pimp and scuttled hurriedly away. The furtive little man was followed out by the fat whore in the now crumpled and stinking see-through blouse. She looked exhausted and slumped down on the steps. The pimp gave her a cigarette that smelt sweet when she lit it.

"Won't be a mo," the pimp said to the fat whore as she inhaled greedily. He squeezed her left breast hard until she looked him in the eye with distaste. "Be good, hun," he smiled at her. "Be really good."

The philosopher pimp led the woman down a narrow alley between two tall houses. The officer following the woman emerged from his hiding place and crossed to the fat whore, who resignedly gave him a drag from her sweetly scented cigarette. He ran his hand between her fleshy legs, sticky with semen, before following the pimp and the woman down the dark alleyway. The fat whore made an obscene but languorous gesture at his back. Then she lay back against the wall, closed her eyes and smoked until anything she had ever thought or felt faded from her mind and was finally forgotten.

Security must be watertight

In the downstairs hall of the Police Commissioner's splendid mansion, the ambitious young businessman sipped his gin and wondered where his little bride could be. She had last been spotted ascending the staircase with the Commissioner's wife. Flattering, of course, but that was ages ago. He hoped his little bride hadn't become emotional. She sometimes did. She sometimes, for no apparent reason, wept and refused to show her face. He hoped she wasn't weeping on the Commissioner's wife's spiky bosom.

He looked around him. Everyone was here. Literally everyone. Well, some weren't, of course. That little alderman and his fruity wife didn't seem to have made it, for some reason. The ambitious young businessman had particularly noticed them as an ill-matched couple. And moreover the alderman had not looked well. Positively green, in fact. He was past it, of course. Yesterday's man. Well, he certainly wouldn't be missed tonight. Time for such as the alderman to make way for new blood. The ambitious businessman's breast swelled at the thought.

And then there was the band. He had heard rumours that the Commissioner's wife had particularly wanted the band to appear but their manager had pleaded a prior engagement. He, the clued-in young businessman, could guess what that was. Still, personally speaking he didn't miss the band's presence. Dangerous anarchists they were, in his humble opinion, preaching their nihilism as if it was entertainment. He listened to the words of the songs, he heard what they were saying: it wasn't lost on him, oh no, it didn't fly over his head. The ambitious young businessman prided himself on being clued in to what was going on. That cop, for example, standing discreetly beside a pillar watching the guests' every move from behind an impenetrable mask. It was reassuring, really. After all, the Commissioner was a prime target and there had been threats. There had been threats against all of them. He had even received one himself, which in a weak moment he had showed to his little bride with a degree of pride. Of course, she had panicked and made a scene which would have been very embarrassing if there had been witnesses.

Nevertheless, with the cream of the cream of the city present tonight — the pillars of society, the bastions of industry, politicians, judges, fire chiefs, millionaires, ambitious businessmen, young and older — it was essential that security should be watertight. The ambitious young businessman took another sip of his gin and bitter tonic and accosted an important and ambitious young stockbroker.

The cop they called Mirandolo watched it all from behind his mask and smiled grimly to himself. Soon, soon.

Geisha

In the soft and silky, black and purple bedroom, the Commissioner's wife scraped at black satin sheets. Her yellow eyes were fixed on the two-way mirror into the shower where the little bride was washing herself scrupulously, all her crevices, all her odorous nooks and crannies. The little bride frequently looked at herself in the mirror, apparently pleased with what she saw, childishly narcissistic. She soaped her armpits, her breasts, her buttocks, her belly. The Commissioner's wife, scraping hard, longed to go in to her now, to make those little baby blues pop out of their sockets again. But after all, anticipation was ninety per cent of pleasure. She could wait. The whole endless night was ahead of them.

A few moments later, the little bride came out of the shower wrapped in the fluffy towel. She glanced at her reflection in the long wall a mirror. It looked good. She was also glad to see the Commissioner's wife now almost decently draped in a long and silky plum-coloured robe.

"I'll have my shower now, lovely," said the Commissioner's predatory wife. "I've put out some of my dresses. Try them on. See which one is you, darling, then I'll fix your hair and face."

Thus it was, at last at last, the ambitious young businessman looked up and saw the Commissioner's wife descend the stairs again in a dress of lime green, high at the neck in front, but slashed down at the back. She was accompanied by a doll, a self-conscious doll in a short bubble-net skirt of flaming orange with a saffron yellow fitted top that pushed up her young breasts to make them look as if they were being offered on a plate.

The doll had, after all, not chosen the outfit herself but had been pressed to it, and she always liked, where possible, to please. The doll's hair was charmingly curled, with tiny yellow and orange bows. Her face was almost geisha-like in its artifice — white powder, rosebud lips, expertly and finely black-edged eyes that looked ever so slightly frightened. For the Commissioner's wife had sighed so much as she rubbed perfumed cream into the little bride's skin. She had shuddered as she stared close into the little bride's eyes, applying the lipstick and mascara, putting her brown and leathery face so close the little bride could smell her shuddering breath.

And now the ambitious young businessman failed to recognise her and thought that the doll was another protégé, his little bride having been abandoned weeping somewhere upstairs. And he turned away in disgust from the doll, while she thought that he must know — as she did, without knowing exactly what — that something wrong had happened. But the Commissioner's wife dragged her to him in pride and said to him, "Congratulations. She's a work of art."

Then he turned and looked into familiar frightened blue eyes and was not sure, after all, whether he was pleased. And the other men present, bastions of industry, pillars of society, fire chiefs, stockbrokers, young and old, gazed at the ambitious young businessman's doll of a little bride, her breasts, her legs, the two inches of milky flesh between her yellow fitted top and her flaming orange skirt, and grinned at each other and winked and salivated. Only the valet, behind a pillar, near the cop, looked on with pity and sorrow.

"Soon," the cop they called Mirandolo muttered to him. "Soon."

Down

The piper was finally tired. His arms and legs felt heavy, as if he were dragging weights that had nothing to do with him. His head was heavy. How long since he had slept? Was it yesterday, today or tomorrow? The day after tomorrow, perhaps. Black clouds hung down over him, pressing on his head, his eyelids. The clouds wrapped him in a soft and inky web. He yawned a great yawn that turned him inside out. He swallowed himself. Down and down and dark and dark. He fell into a doorway and into an immediate and impenetrable sleep. And over his head, the exotic birds which had followed him everywhere, hovered and chirruped and whistled.

The Little White Sisters of the Immaculate Mother, not to mention the Big Brown Brothers of the Day of Wrath, now rising from their hard beds to go and pray that the cup should pass from them, or that they should have the strength to endure it, would no longer have recognised Brother Joachim praying as never before, in the knowledge that he must drain the cup to its dregs, that he would have the strength to endure. His white and skinny body, stripped of ladies' garments and resembling now nothing so much as the figure of Christ in a Gothic pieta, had been bound with thin wire that bit through his skin.

But there had been worse. As the demonic compere leapt and capered in his crimson costume and jeered and poured out remembered venom of childhood punishments, as the vicious Lucifer poked and spat at his erstwhile teacher, the terrible and filthy gypsy had forced his prestidigitator's fingers into Joachim's mouth and ripped out his tongue.

"No more rivers," Lucifer had screeched in a frenzy, "no more mountains, no more cities, no more lakes, no more seas, no more deserts..."

After a while, Brother Joachim had almost got used to the pain, and after another while the blood stopped gushing. He could endure it. But then there was worse. His ex-pupil crept up to him and caressed his blood-soaked chest and wiped the blood away so tenderly and wept and chuckled and all the time told him, told him, until Joachim wished they had deafened him, too. And then they wished they had blinded him.

"You'll never guess what," Lucifer was whispering. "You'll never guess what I've got. Guess, go on." He poked Joachim in the belly. "He gave it to me." He pointed at the grinning, filthy gypsy. Spattered also with Joachim's blood. "Look at him, the filthy bugger. Would you let that filthy bugger bugger you, miss? Well, I did, over and over again, screaming with pleasure, and he gave me a wonderful present. He gave me... Guess! He gave me... Guess?"

But how could brother Joachim guess, fainting with pain, and if he guessed, how could he speak?

The little creature hopped and leapt and danced around, clapping his hands.

"He gave me.... Death... I'm dying. I'm dying. You don't believe me? You do believe me? Yes, it's true. No more rivers, no more lakes, no more mountains, no more deserts, no more seas. Nothing. Nothing."

His hollow black eyes looked at Joachim exultantly.

"And now we're going to pass the present on. Aren't we?"

The gypsy grinned bloodily.

Joachim could endure it. Now he could endure it.

"No love, not you," the little compere said, tapping him playfully. "You're too old to die young. I wouldn't dream of giving you an easy way out. In any case, to be perfectly honest none of us would touch you with the proverbial barge-pole, even if we happened to have one about us. You looked bad enough before, miss. I may call you miss, mayn't I? But now... Honey, you just don't have what it takes. Still, never call me hard-hearted. I'll tell you what. I'll let you watch."

The compere skipped out and returned a moment later pulling the golden boy after him. The golden boy looked at Joachim in horror.

"Don't worry, darling," sang the little compere merrily, "Miss begged us to do it to her. Mortification of the flesh, don't you know. She's a monk, a kink. I should know. She taught me geography for five years. She spanked the capital cities of the world into my bare bum. And now, you know what, I can't remember a single one. I couldn't tell you the name of single capital city, not even our own. Isn't that a hoot? Not a river, not a mountain, not a sea. Despite all that spanking. Well, sister won't be doing any spanking any more. That's one certain thing in this uncertain life." The compere addressed Joachim, stroking the boy. "Now miss, isn't he beautiful? Have you ever seen anything so beautiful? And he's all mine. He was given to me as a present. So now, fair's fair, I'm going to give him a present too. Well, not me, exactly. I'm not up to it. Him." The giggling ex-pupil pointed to the filthy gypsy.

And while Joachim struggled and groaned and moaned, the filthy gypsy touched the golden boy. And as Joachim struggled, the wire cut further into his flesh and drew blood. The terrible sounds that emerged from his mouth could not be translated into any known language.

And the golden boy screamed too.

"He really is a virgin," the compere remarked with satisfaction. "They usually aren't, you know. They usually pretend. Anyway this darling," (the boy was still screaming) "is most definitely a virgin. Either that or an awfully good actor."

He tore his gaze from the entrancing scene for a moment to look again deep into Joachim's eyes. Joachim, looking back, felt that he was falling into a black pit, the unspeakable pit of the compere's eyes.

"You know," the compere was saying to him, "You've been quite wrong all along. There is no God. There is no God. There is no God."

A freak like us

The piper dreamt of a time a long time before, when a child trod a crunching path of silver shells on an endless beach. He walked and walked and when he turned back his mamma had become small, an unrecognisable dot among other dots. He dreamt of a time before time, when a child had run into a cave and round deep pools with steep sides, waving with green weed and stones with secret places where crabs hid, where a wooden crate with the name of distant port crudely painted on it was floating empty. And the walls of the cave were wet and stalactites hung from the roof and it soon became too dark to see anything, and soon there was no light, and no amount of standing in the dark could get you used to it, for there was no light. And the child had wept for his mamma who had been a tiny indistinguishable dot and who now had disappeared completely.

And the child opened his eyes in the dark and out of the rocky walls strange figures closed in on him, and he screamed for his mamma, but she was nowhere. And the piper drew back into the dark recess of the doorway. But there was no escape from the strange figures who closed in on him.

"Friend," said the dwarf. "Friend, friend."

"Hello, there," replied the piper, waking. "How are you?"

"We want a word with you, friend."

The strange figures stepped forward.

"Yes?"

"It's about our darlin girl, our angel."

A sigh went up from the strange figures.

"Who would that be?" the piper asked.

"Who do you think? Not her, for a start." The dwarf pointed at the bearded lady. "Our little Snow White, of course."

"Oh?" the piper asked. "What's happened to her?"

"Haven't you heard?" a woman midget asked.

"She's gone," the dwarf said.

"You mean," the piper smiled in a friendly fashion, "she just upped and went."

"Oh no, friend, nothing like that."

"Nothing like that," squeaked Rodolpho.

"She couldn't of done that. Not by herself."

"She's helpless without us, see."

"We understands her needs, see."

"Her very perticoolar needs." The dwarf put his long pale face down close to the piper, who smelt the rose-scented breath.

"Well, maybe after all, the handsome prince came to waken her with a kiss," laughed the piper.

"No handsome prince," replied the dwarf, not moving. "They don't exist. That's all a fairytale, friend."

"More like," the woman midget stared severely at the piper, "a thief in the night."

"She won't wake up, you know," the dwarf said. "Not never, she won't."

"How do you know?" asked the piper, "Maybe the...stimuli... have been wrong."

"We've tried everything."

"Mention it, we've tried it."

"I don't think so," the piper replied meaningfully, knowing that he was treading dangerous ground. "I very much doubt it. After all, it's not in your interest, is it. I wouldn't be surprised if you haven't given her something to make her sleep. I wouldn't be surprised to hear that you've hypnotised her."

The strange creatures looked at him blankly.

"Now whyever would we do that, friend?" asked the dwarf.

"It stands to reason, doesn't it." The piper wanted to keep talking, his tongue suddenly silver. "She's your main attraction. Bearded ladies have had their day and limbless men have a limited appeal. Strong men are two a penny, as for female contortionists — forget it! But Snow White, she's an enigma. People come back again and again to see her. She's worth a lot of money to you."

"You think money is our chief consideration, then, eh?" The dwarf was truly amazed.

"I suppose she could fake it for you," the piper went on. "If she wanted. But she wouldn't want to, would she. One look at you lot and she'd scarper as fast as she could."

"You got it all worked out, ain't you," the dwarf commented venomously.

"You'd have nothing beautiful to look at any more. You'd have to start looking at each other again."

"We want her back," the woman midget said softly.

The strange creatures pushed forwards until they were almost on top of the piper.

"We know you took her."

"Where have you hidden her?"

"Thought you could fool us, did you?"

"Give her back now and no more will be said on the matter."

"Give her back!" the piper shouted, struggling to his feet. "So that you can continue violating her in front of a gaping crowd!"

"You understand nothin," the dwarf shouted back.

"What is there to understand?" cried the piper. "I love her."

At this the strange creatures contorted with laughter into even stranger shapes. The piper looked at them in dread.

"Oh hoho," the dwarf Mishka wiped his streaming eyes on his sleeve, "that's it. Eh? You love her. Wonderful. True love, is it? Eh, eh? What's that mean, eh? You got some romantic notion in your silly noddle about her? She's pretty, so you love her. She's a mystery, a ninigma, so you love her. She's unobtainable, so you love her... Ha!" the dwarf poked his finger into the piper's chest, driving him back against the wall. "You don't know what love is, fool."

"And I suppose you know all about it," the piper countered.

"Yes," the dwarf said. "We do. The ugly and unwanted know what love really is. And we really love her. Give her back to us."

"Give her back to us."

"Give her back to us."

"Give her back to us."

"She needs us," the woman midget said.

"Need, need! I need her," the piper cried.

"Have you fed her?"

"Changed her knickers?"

"She shits too, like everyone else."

"I'll never give her back," shouted the piper. "Never. Not to you, you disgusting freaks."

The strange creatures hissed and gasped. Then the dwarf whispered very softly, "But she's a freak, too, friend. A freak like us."

"No no no no no..."

"Of course she is," the dwarf whispered. "Did you think she weren't?"

The piper covered his face.

"Please give her back," pleaded the woman midget.

"Please," they all said.

"We need her," said the woman midget. "Her fiancé needs her."

The piper looked up, gaping.

"Her fiancé?"

The strange creatures pushed forward the dejected figure of the ugly midget, head bowed, dragging the broom that once upon a time had served him as a horse.

"Him!"

"Did you really think," the dwarf said softly, "that we'd let just anyone touch her like that. She's wearing his ring."

The piper groaned a terrible agony.

"No," he moaned, "it's too grotesque to imagine."

He made as if to break out of the circle of strange creatures but they held him back, pummelling him in their fury, catching at his clothes, the chocolate and banana-coloured hound's tooth jacket once belonging to the last husband, the dead tourist's white linen trousers.

Then the exotic birds that had been hovering over his head, that had been following him everywhere since he started playing, plucked the piper naked out of the attacking circle and carried him away over the city, away to safety.

The strange creatures watched his flight, his silver body gleaming like a sliver of moonlight.

"Don't worry," the dwarf comforted the ugly midget. "He'll lead us to her soon. Don't worry."

Finished

The canvasses stood propped higgledy-piggledy round the Commissioner's office, the artist gazing at her work enraptured. She was as exhausted as if she had just given birth to seven children. Seven pictures. Fruit of her body.

The dead tourist's bones lay still now on the desk but in a strange new configuration. They pointed to a button on the Commissioner's desk. They surrounded the button, all pointing at it. The artist pressed the button.

Away across the dark city in his glittering mansion, packing his cheeks with the flesh of both black and white swan, with truffles and oysters, with eel, with baby calf cooked in its mother's milk, with steak tartar and raw egg — his wife could always be relied on at least to provide a good spread — the Commissioner at last became aware of the bleeper bleeping on his belt. Grabbing a blackbird stuffed with cherries in one hand and a couple of avocados with crab in the other, he made his way to a telephone and called his office, preparing to be furious with the inferior who had disregarded his orders not to disturb him on any account. To his surprise and pleasure, he recognised instead the deep voice of the amateur artist like brandied honey and whipped cream.

"I've finished," she breathed.

"I'll come immediately," he replied.

In answer to his wife's beady stare — and how he would have liked to spit in her face, to let the gob of spittle trickle down over that cruel mask — he said, "I have to go. Urgent. Police work."

He clapped the cop they called Mirandolo on the sleeve, intensifying the obnoxious and pungent odour that clung persistently to the clothes of their owner (himself now a heap of charred grease).

"Great work," said the Commissioner, averting his face. "Keep it up."

The Commissioner grabbed a few more titbits — for he wanted to share again with the artist and reward her gastronomically — and shoved them into the pockets of his uniform. He then quietly left the mansion to his wife and guests and squeezed into the official limousine that stood always ready. Not before he had spotted what looked like a silver man held up by birds flying over the city.

"Ha!" he said, and blamed the lobster mousse.

The artist, naked and multicoloured, her sweat having run the paints all over her body, her rainbow hair hanging round her heavy face, was meanwhile clambering up the stairs to the bright high room, in her hands the dead tourist's two thigh bones that vibrated in her grasp. Up and up and up.

Beginner's luck

The philosopher pimp jerked his head towards a filthy café, where mask-faced women flicked soiled boas at them as they entered.

"But I've been here before," said the woman remembering. "Surely this isn't the place."

"It's as good a place as any," the philosopher pimp said and he winked at shadowy figures seated at tables in the corners of the filthy café and made rapid hand movements behind the woman's back.

"But is he here?" the woman asked. "I paid you, remember."

"The fact of the matter is, darlin," the pimp said in a friendly manner, "I haven't fuckin clue where he is."

And he, the wad of money wedged into his tight green silk trousers, skipped off into the night, passing as he went, a little old crone not worth a moment's attention, who gasped as he passed and pointed something briefly at him. Passing, too, a man in a raincoat whom he recognised as a cop. But a cop on the take. No worries there either.

The woman sank down exhausted at a filthy table. There was no sign, at least, of the old woman in the crooked ginger wig.

A shadowy figure crossed over to her. At that moment, one of the women with the soiled boas jumped on to the bar and started crooning softly to herself, started dancing in a provocative way, started stripping.

"Yes?" the woman asked the shadowy figure. Just a man after all, with a pock-scarred face.

"Yes?" he asked.

"Do you know where he is?" she asked. "Mr El Blanco."

"Of course I do, lovely."

"Will you take me to him?"

"With pleasure."

She stood up and took his arm because she was shaking with tiredness and could not stand alone. She let herself be led from the filthy café where the woman dancing on the bar was pulling the soiled boa between her legs, tickling her genitals with it in sham ecstasy. No one seemed to be paying her any attention.

The shadowy figure took the woman away down another endless street, down another steaming alleyway. They came to a dead end.

"Here?" she asked uncertainly, seeing no door in the high surrounding walls.

"Here," the man said.

She turned then and saw the others. Two other men, shadowy in the dark.

"He'll be along," the first man said.

"You must of just missed him," said the second.

"What's so special about him, anyway?" asked the third.

"Won't we do?" We can help you pass the time."

"While you're waiting, like."

They circled her.

"Keep away from me," the woman said.

"Looking for a good time?" the third man — or was it the second? — asked softly.

"You've come to the right place," the second man — or was it the first? — whispered.

"We know how to give a girl a really good time."

A shadowy figure pinned her to the wall. She tasted his blubbery mouth. He ripped the purse from around her neck and threw it to another shadowy figure. Who looked at the contents and whistled.

"My, my, you must be looking for a real good time."

"No," the woman spluttered. "You've got the money. You can go now. I don't want anything. You've got it wrong."

"Us," a man pressed against her. "Oh no, pussycat. We never get it wrong."

"It's you that's got it wrong, baby."

"Oh so wrong."

"No one comes looking for Mr El Blanco. See."

"It's most unlikely that you'd have anything he'd want."

"But you never know."

"You might be lucky."

"Wonders never cease. That's what they say."

"We've heard that said."

"I... I only wanted to ask him a question," the woman murmured.

"Don't we all, sugarplum."

"We're all looking for the answers to our questions."

"But," the first man caressed her hair and then tugged it hard, forcing her head back, "it won't do, you know, coming after him."

"Not waiting," the second man pulled at her breasts, forcing her to her knees, "for him to send for you."

"Apparently," the third man said, striking her face, "you didn't know that."

"But we're willing," the first man said, kicking her back on to the wet ground, "to give you the benefit of the doubt. Aren't we, lads."

"Oh sure we are."

"But..." said the third man.

"But..." said the second man.

"But just to make sure the lesson gets learnt real well," said the first man, smiling greasily at her.

"Good and proper."

"Just," said the first man, "to make sure you never come looking again."

"Never."

"Not ever."

"It's necessary," the first man said, lifting her skirt with the toe of his boot, "to... rub it in a bit... like."

"The lesson, that is," said the third man, unbuckling his belt.

"Baby," said the second man.

"Sugarplum," said the third man.

"Pussycat," said the first man.

As the woman started screaming and remembering, an old crone stumbled down the alleyway waving something in her hand. No one paid any attention to her, an old crone like her. But as the woman continued to scream as the memories came back at last, the old crone fired three shots into the backs of the shadowy figures hovering over the woman. Just three shots — **BANG BANG BANG** — and three men slumped dead, for the old crone, never having fired a gun before in her life, had beginner's luck and hit each man through to the heart.

In the glass room

The room was round, with a domed ceiling. It was made entirely of glass. The light in the room was ultra violet, so that anything white gleamed luminously. It made the bandage that was being wrapped round the body of the singer gleam luminously. The singer was standing on a plinth, staring through heavy eyes at the domed glass ceiling of the room that looked out at the endless night. She couldn't have told how long she had been standing there, almost motionless, arms held away from her body so that the white bandage could be wrapped around her.

Somewhere out there in the night he could be watching her, through his reflecting glasses. She knew he often watched when she didn't know, she didn't know why. She didn't know why there was suddenly this passion for bandages, gold, black, white. They were bound tightly round her body, as though she were a corpse, a mummy, only gaps were left in strange places for brown flesh to show through. The white bandages were being wrapped tightly above her breasts so that naked they projected sharply through, above her belly, below her belly, tight above her buttocks, tight below them, tight around her thighs.

She stood and gazed up at the endless night through heavy smoky eyes. She could not have told how long she had been standing there. She didn't know whether the man was watching her. She didn't care. Once there had been two children. Once, long ago, or she had dreamed it. But it didn't seem to matter.

She felt sharp pain as silver clips were fixed to her nipples. Looking down at last, she saw how her breasts projected through the bandages, how star-shaped silver clips had been fixed to her nipples, pinching them.

"You look beautiful, darling," the old woman in the crooked ginger wig told her, lifting the heavy black hair and fixing it in place with combs that bit into the scalp. "You always look beautiful."

At that moment, above them, above the glass dome of the glass room, the silver-skinned piper floated naked, held by exotic birds. Both women looked up but he didn't look down at them. His eyes were fixed on the window of a spidery house far across the city, where a princess lay sleeping among reflections and whispers.

The miracle

It was of course a miracle that nothing had been taken. Everyone, nuns and monks and priests agreed. The door of the cathedral had split in two. Anyone could have crept up the aisle under the gaze of none but the plaster saints, could have slid over the marble floor to the altar with its priceless gold-embossed tabernacle containing chalice and ciborium, the crucifix worked with rubies and emeralds, sapphires and amethyst, the solid gold monstrance whose crystal chamber contained a splinter of the true cross. The possibilities didn't bear thinking about.

A guard nevertheless would have to be placed over the treasures before high mass. Then the treasures would have to be removed to a place of safety until the doors had been fixed.

The doors! Was it vandalism? Was it lightning? No vandal could have done such a thing. There had been no lightning. Clearly the devil was walking the streets of the city on this unnatural endless night. The devil had tried to enter the cathedral to desecrate it. And having tried once, assuredly he would try again.

Look what you've done

"Fuck!" yelled the raincoated cop who had been following the woman. "Fuck!" he yelled, pulling at the three bodies on top of her. "You stupid cunt. Look what you've done now."

He dragged the woman out from under the three no longer shadowy, all too corporeal bodies. Fuck! He pulled her out and started slapping her about the face and head.

"You stupid cunt. Don't you know what you've done? We're both dead."

The woman dropped moaning to her knees as this strange man continued to hit her. She didn't know why he was hitting her. She didn't know why the three men attacking her had suddenly dropped dead across her body. Had this man shot them to save her? She started kissing his hands.

"Stop that, you stupid bitch," he caught her viciously in the ribs with his boot. He wanted to kick her to death. She had killed him.

Then — he wasn't after all very bright — he remembered the other one. The old crone with the gun. Where the fuck had she wandered off to? He looked around. No sign of her. Fuck! He ran down the alleyway and looked along the road. Nothing in any direction. He ran back to grab the woman before she made off, too. She was staggering towards him. He grabbed her arm and dragged her after him, though she could hardly walk. Although one of her shoes fell off, he pulled her fast after him.

"Where's your pal, eh? Where's she gone, eh? Not talking, eh? You'll talk soon enough down at the station. You think you've felt pain. You don't know what pain is, sister. But you're going to find out."

He dragged her past steaming drains, past blazing buildings, past a sad-faced procession of dwarfs and midgets, passing — had she been in a fit state to notice — a spidery house breathing the regular breath of deep sleep, past sinister basements, past the cold and empty cathedral with its cracked open doors, past the melted down concert hall, a fountain with red rods rising, a café collapsed deep into an abyss in the earth. Neither the woman nor the raincoated officer noticing. Neither thinking it was strange.

He dragged her at last into the square, past the table where the dead tourist had been sitting, past the head of the dead tourist peeping out just then from under another table, past a mother wheeling a pram silently, her feet tick-tocking on the pavement of the empty square. He dragged her up the now familiar steps of the police station, up to where the officer sat at his desk as if he had been waiting all his life for her to arrive.

Mary Immaculata

God have mercy on us! God protect and defend us!

Had the devil after all entered the cathedral? The shocking discovery had been made appropriately enough by Sister Mary Immaculata when she entered Our Lady's Chapel to offer up prayers for the deliverance of the city from the dreadful night. When she raised her eyes and saw that the statue of Our Lady was gone.

The Little White Sisters blessed themselves over and over and prayed fervently that no blasphemy had been intended, that misplaced piety was to blame. The statue, after all, had no value as an artefact, being of a standard, mass-produced plaster variety, seen in a thousand churches and grottoes. It's only value would surely be to a true believer. That's what the Little White Sisters fervently hoped and prayed, that no devil-worshipper — and devil-worshippers surely abounded on such an endless night — had stolen her to take part in some obscene ritual.

Freezing

The birds had finally taken the piper up on to the mountain again. Maybe their instinct told them that was where he wanted to be, away from the dangerous city. The birds dropped the piper gently on to the harsh grass of the mountaintop. Then they perched around him, waiting. He still held the tin whistle. Now he would surely play.

The piper shivered. The city had been hot but here the air had grown chill. The fires had gone out. People had lost faith in the power of fire and in any case there was nothing left to burn. The piper was naked and cold. He hunted around for discarded clothes but there was nothing. Everything had been burnt. People on the mountain, naked, unconscious, were freezing to death. He would have to take his chance in the city again. He would have, in any case, to return to Snow White.

Limping, pallid, the piper started wearily to clamber down the rocks for the third time on that endless night.

The formalities have to be observed

The party was going with a swing. Of course it was. The Commissioner's wife had a gift for giving parties. Everyone told her so. You have a gift, they said. And she smiled a ghastly death's head smile.

Who was this bitch with the big tits, anyway? Where was her usual languid maid? (Lying in a coma in the handpicked valet's bedroom). The valet had told her that the languid maid had suddenly gone home to her parents' house in the country and that this fat-arsed bitch was the best he could get at the last minute. That wasn't organisation: that was mismanagement.

Well, she'd tear the little cow's sleepy eyes out if ever she came back. Didn't she know when she was well off? As for this hippopotamus, after tonight she could wobble back to whatever zoo she had escaped from.

The full-breasted woman smiled at the men as she handed round the snacks. Eat them if you like, her eyes seemed to say, but I'm a tastier dish. And the men smiled back and their eyes seemed to say, apologetically of course, I'd rather eat you and maybe later I will, but just for the present the formalities have to be observed.

The Commissioner's wife smiled sweetly at the judge who was telling her that she had a gift for giving parties. He had just extracted from the full-breasted maid a promise to meet him in the pantry.

The ambitious businessman's little bride was in the centre of a group of admirers, who were forcing titbits on her. Once she dropped a crystallised cherry on to her breast and quick as a flash a banking magnate licked it up.

Her young husband could get nowhere near her. He tried to catch her eye but her lids were weighted down with false lashes and she kept closing them, hoping that soon, soon, she would wake up, safely tucked up in her own little bed.

The ambitious young businessman felt a claw scrape at his neck.

"Enjoying yourself?" the Commissioner's wife breathed at him.

"Oh yes, very much. Thank you."

He was a good-looking young man, who took care of his body in the belief that physical fitness was essential in order to get ahead.

"You're in perfect condition, aren't you?" The Commissioner's wife sucked at his ear, her yellow eyes gleaming.

"I believe in keeping in trim."

"I couldn't agree more. I'm the same way myself."

The ambitious young businessman looked at her. It was true: the Commissioner's wife certainly had an exceptional body for a woman of her age.

"I have some equipment upstairs," she went on. "Perhaps you would like to try it out."

"I would indeed," the young businessman answered politely.

"Come on then," she smiled. He saw her large teeth, the glint in her yellow eyes. "Now?"

"Face it, darling, you're bored to death." She drew his hand and pressed it to her hard chest. "Come on. A work-out would do you good."

The young businessman felt that ambition impelled him to go where inclination balked. This was a woman of almost legendary power. He allowed himself to be drawn. They passed the rotting flower arrangement, its stench intensified by strong perfume. The young businessman gazed at it in horror. Beads of black blood, revitalised by decay, dripped down it. But the Commissioner's wife drew him on, up the stairs. The ambitious young businessman looked back. No one noticed. No one. Above all, not his doll-like little bride, pawed and squeezed by surreptitious hands, her eyes closed now, her mouth fixed in a painted smile.

Too long have I waited

Brother Joachim thought he must have passed out, for how long he did not know. The room was empty, there was no sound from the club beyond. Blood no longer flowed from his mouth but his feet were numb and he could see that where the wire was tightest on his ankles, they were turning blue. His hands, too, behind him, had no feeling in them.

But physical suffering was the least of his worries. Mortification of the flesh, the impious imp had said. And not far wrong at that. Did not Brother Joachim bear even now faintly on the palm of his left hand the stigmatus, mark of the enthusiasm of his youth, when in the throes of a mystical ecstasy he had driven a spike through his hand in emulation of the Lord Jesus Christ? Had he not worn next to his skin for many years a hair shirt that scratched and irritated and drew blood? Physical pain he could stand more than most men. But the other thing. No God, the horrible hobgoblin had said. There is no God. Clearly this was a devil sent to tempt him. Only, only... in Brother Joachim's darkest moods, in his happiest moods, when the world seemed to dance before his eyes and paradise was surely here and now and not in some obscure future as a reward to children for being obedient and good, Brother Joachim had occasionally thought the same thing. There is no God. Man has made God. Man is God.

Over the centuries, people had called on a deity. In their pain and in their joy. But never, never once had there been an answer. Children crying for comfort had been left bereft. Joachim tried to cry but merely managed to grunt. So he would die here, like this, and the brothers would have another scandal to hush up.

He almost smiled at the thought. If he could, he would have smiled at the thought of Father Remedios being brought to him here, to identify him, perhaps. Someone, Goodfellow no doubt, had tied the rose pink padded bra again round him again, like an obscene blasphemy. All Joachim had ever wanted was the gentleness that is in women, that he once thought was in women. Before his tear-filled eyes sprang an image of the Mother of God as she was in the cathedral, as she was in so many churches and grottoes throughout the land, pallid, blue-eyed, coral-lipped, forgiving, meek and mild. He tried to move his lips in prayer. It was always easier to talk to the Mother than to the Father. The Mother who listened and forgave. The Father who judged and punished.

Then suddenly there she actually was in the room before him, dressed in the customary white and blue, the colours of purity. There she was, Mary the Mother, her blue eyes burning with rage at the sight of him.

"Has it come to this?" she cried in a shrill voice. "Were we locked away all these years until it came to this?"

She strode angrily about the room, her robes flapping round her.

"They never told us things had come so far. I have seen such things this endless night. They cannot be forgiven," she said suddenly, ripping her cowl from her head and spreading it over him. "Vengeance is near. Too long have I waited. They killed my son, you know. Of course you know. Everyone knows. But didn't you ever wonder why I let them? Heh? I let them because I thought things would change. Imagine that! How stupid can you get! And of course they continue to kill, sons and daughters. Mothers, fathers, babies. Millions have perished violently. In his name." She pointed over her head. "I cannot stand by and watch any longer. I cannot forgive any longer."

Wild-eyed, wild-haired, she stood there shaking her fist at the silent God. Joachim cowered in terror, waiting for the thunderbolt.

"You too," she shouted, pointing at him, "will be avenged." And out she raced, her hair streaming behind her. Had Joachim not felt the soft cloth on his body, he would have doubted whether she had ever been there at all. He wondered why she had not paused to undo his bonds before leaving him so precipitously. It would after all only have taken a moment. If she had loosed his bonds, he could have done his own avenging. Though actually all he wanted now was to find the golden boy, tarnished now but perhaps not lost, and take him away from this terrible place to safety. With this thought, Joachim jerked against the wire bonds which seared his flesh with such agony that he passed out again.

Don't be afraid

The stringy policewoman listened carefully at the door. The sobs had stopped. The boy had been sobbing for hours, but now, for hours, had been silent. Maybe he was sleeping. Children sleep easily, the stringy policewoman thought enviously. She never slept, or only with the aid of stronger and stronger doses of morphine. In fact, she could do with some now. Not to sleep, of course, just to relax. The boy wouldn't try to escape. He wasn't the stuff that the artist woman was made of. He was a foolish and terrified boy who would wait, shitting himself until they came to take him away. Surely she could leave him safely for a few moments. She would only be a few moments.

The stringy policewoman slipped down a few flights of stairs and into the locker room. She opened her locker and took a package from the back of it. Then she went to the ladies' lavatory. No one was about. In the privacy of a cubicle, she shot liquid nirvana into her scarred thigh.

Up, up past the locker room went the naked artist. The bones of the dead tourist trembled in her hand. Up to the once bright room, now plunged in darkness. The door was locked and the key was gone but the artist knocked with the bones on the door of the once bright room and the door sprang open.

Light flooding in behind her threw the Circean figure of the artist into silhouette. The rookie policeman, cowering in a corner, cried out in terror. The artist noticed how lines of suffering were now carved on to his young face.

"Don't be afraid," she said in her soft and deep voice. "Come with me."

The rookie policeman was afraid but less afraid at the sound of her soft voice than he had been at the sight of her naked and pagan form.

"I will save you," she said. "I won't harm you. Be quick, for she will soon return."

The young policeman made for the door.

"Not that way," the artist said. "They will catch you and shoot you. Come with me."

Now the rookie policeman could see her eyes and sank into them. The artist led him to the window that looked out over the city, over the dark lump of the mountain, across the endless plain towards the sea. She tapped the dead tourist's bones lightly on the window, which shattered into diamond shards. The artist, leading, climbed through the window and the boy, unafraid now, followed her. They stood on the roof, feeling with pleasure the rising wind brush their flesh. At that moment, the stringy policewoman floated back up the stairs to find the door open and her captive gone.

"No!" she screamed, rushing into the room. "No!" she screamed, gripping the edge of the broken window, her hands ripped, as she saw the two figures perched like birds on the roof. "No!" she screamed, as they stepped off the roof together. She scrambled out of the window, over the roof, almost losing her footing. She peered over the edge of the roof and saw the wild woman who was once an amateur artist and the boy who was once a rookie policeman floating down on the breeze and landing lightly in the square below.

Then the stringy policewoman saw the wild woman strike the high gratings of the dungeon cells that looked out into the square so that the gratings fell in, and she saw criminals and political prisoners, prostitutes, protesters and felons, an old tramp in a linen jacket with a bloodstained rip across the back, squeeze out through the impossibly narrow spaces and rush off in all directions, away to freedom. And the wild woman and the boy sauntered off arm in arm as well, while the stringy policewoman shouted obscenities after them until they were gone from her sight.

She clambered back with difficulty into the once bright room, shards of glass sticking into her. And down she staggered to the locker room again. Again she opened the door of her locker and took from the back a package. And this time she didn't bother to go to the ladies' lavatory but there and then forced enough drug into her thigh to ensure that she would never have difficulty sleeping again.

Below in the square, now with no one to see except a mother wheeling a pram, tick tock, tick tock, the official limousine of the police department drove up to the door, and the Commissioner bounced out, his pockets bulging, a grin on his face. Bounced out and in and up the stairs to his office.

Some mistake

On another floor, in a soundproof and windowless room, two officers were interrogating the woman.

"Where did you say," the once seated officer was asking the officer who had been tailing the woman, "where did you say you picked up this whore, officer?"

"Near the Street of Innocents, sir."

"The Street of Innocents, eh." He laughed unpleasantly. "Nice place for a mother, I must say. Very nice indeed. Or have you changed your tune, eh? Eh?" He buffeted her playfully. "Are you still playing that washed out old tune, eh?"

The woman writhed. "It's the truth."

This time the officer belted her across the face.

"Bitch!" he spat. "Don't think I don't know. You can't pull the wool over my eyes. What sort of idiots do you think you're dealing with, eh" (BELT) "Eh?"

"We're up to your tricks," the second officer said, so far having kept out of it.

"I don't know what you're talking about," the woman gasped.

The first officer crouched down and whispered wetly in her ear.

"You're with them, aren't you, the terrorists, the Black Death crowd," he said. "You're one of them. Don't give me any more spiel. We know all about it. We've had you under surveillance for some time. Isn't that right?"

"Every move." The second officer spat on the floor.

"So you see," the first officer put his arm round the woman's shoulders — God! she was bony! — "no need to pretend any more. Just give me the details of the plot."

"What?"

"The conspiracy, the next stage. We know there's a concerted plan by you and yours to undermine the fabric of society. All I want..." he nuzzled her neck. She shuddered. "All I want is names and dates and places."

The woman felt his hand slither round and grip her breast.

"There's some mistake." She knew it was useless.

But the first officer, feeling cosy, didn't get angry straight away. He massaged her nipple, feeling her body grow slack.

"Our inside sources," he whispered as though the words were sweet nothings, "have informed us of an assassination attempt against a highly respected member of the community. Need I say more. I can guarantee you immunity from prosecution if you come clean now. Can't say fairer than that, can I?"

"I'm... looking for my daughter," the woman sighed.

The first officer dug his nails into her breast. He threw her to the ground and kicked her viciously in the belly.

"Say that once more and I'll get really nasty," he snarled. "That little pretence is over. Get it. We don't want to hear about it any more. You never had a daughter. No son either."

(Back in the spidery house, a mirror cracked. Someone sobbed. Or was it the rising wind?)

"Please," the woman begged.

"Who thought that one up, eh?" the first officer said, kicking her round the room. "Great cover, they said, great cover for poking your ugly little snout in here, there, everywhere. Didn't work, though, did it? Instead of wiping out one of our foremost and respected citizens, you nearly got wiped out yourself. That's what happens when amateurs get caught up in the big time. Didn't your mam ever tell you, play with matches and you'll get your fingers burnt? Lucky our officer here happened on the spot in time to save you. Do you know how lucky you are?" (KICK) "Do you?" (KICK) "Do you?" (KICK)

"She's not showing much gratitude," the second officer remarked. He was wary. He hadn't yet told his superior about the old crone, nor about the murder of the minions. Maybe the problem would go away. Maybe.

"She's not," the first officer said, "showing much gratitude. Lick my boot."

He stuck his boot in the woman's face. When she refused to lick it, he kicked her in the mouth.

"That's better," he said with satisfaction as she at last ran her tongue over the highly polished leather — these people really had no self-respect — "We can be very responsive to gratitude, can't we."

"Indeed we can," the second officer said meaningfully, hoping the woman wouldn't blurt out anything about the three dead minions. If she did, he would personally chop her hands off.

"But," the first officer was saying, removing his foot — he didn't really want this used-up old whore's saliva all over his nice clean boot, "we can also take ingratitude very badly. Very badly. In fact, I can assure you from my past observation that it would be in your very best interests to co-operate with us now, to save yourself further... inconvenience."

The woman crawled across the floor.

"I don't know what you're talking about," she sobbed. "I really don't. I just want my daughter. Give me back my daughter. I want my daughter."

The first officer looked at her thoughtfully.

"Of course you do," he said, winking at the second officer. "And we're going to take you to her just as soon as you tell us what you know."

"The names of your friends," prompted the second officer. If only he be the first to get to the old crone.

"My friends?" the woman asked stupidly.

"That's all, pet," the first officer said. "And then… you can see your daughter."

The woman looked up at him. The skin around her eyes was purple and puffy.

"You know where she is?"

The first officer smiled down at her.

"We just found her. She's perfectly all right, isn't she, officer."

"Right as rain."

The woman sobbed again.

"Thank God!"

The officer looked at her in distaste. Christ, how he loathed weepers.

"Now about that gratitude," he began.

"Your friends have nothing to fear if they are innocent," the second officer put in.

"The innocent have nothing to fear," the woman said.

"Right you are. Well said. I couldn't have said it better myself."

"Really? " the woman asked radiantly. "She's really here?"

"She's on her way," the first officer said. "They're bringing her over. Just time for you to tell me about your friends."

"There's only one," the woman said. Friends, indeed!

The officers looked at each other. The second officer took out a notebook. It could be the truth. It wouldn't be surprising. That was the way these terrorist groups operated. Small cells. One contact, even. The way to protect the organisation. This woman obviously knew very little. She was unreliable. A weak link. She wouldn't have been told much.

"One friend, eh?" the first officer said. "A lot of people would be glad of even one good friend."

"Yes, he is good," the woman said joyfully. Her daughter! Her daughter! And for a moment she had even wondered.... "But you know," she went on. "I don't even know his name. Isn't that funny?"

The two officers were not particularly amused. "He" the second officer was thinking.

"So what do you know about him, your friend?" the first officer asked.

"Nothing really. He's an artist, though," the woman said. She really knew very little.

"An artist?" the officer prompted, thinking a piss artist. The second officer merely wrote.

"Oh yes. He could have done much better for himself... I mean, playing the tin whistle in the street. What sort of a..."

"The piper, you mean? The one that plays out there all day long. Drives us nutty?"

"Yes, he was helping me search."

"I always thought he was some sort of village idiot," the first officer said.

"He was with her most of the time, up till the end," the second officer put in, as he thought, helpfully.

The first officer looked at him with hatred.

"What!"

"Yeh." The second officer failed to notice the look. "Inseparable they were. Then he went off."

"You arsehole! So where is he now?"

The second officer started thinking slowly. Shit! He was in the shit again.

"Find him," the first officer said. "Alive." Then, to the woman. "And you, piss off."

"My daughter?"

"Clear out!"

"Where is she? You said..."

"Piss off before I change my mind. Your own lot can deal with you, now that you've squealed."

The woman started to scream.

"You said you had my daughter. I want my daughter. Where is she?"

The first officer stepped towards her.

When the rage of the first officer had worn off at last, the woman crawled along the corridors of the police station, not thinking. Not allowing herself to think. Down the stairs into the square, across to the fountain that soon ran red with her blood.

The seed dies that the tree might grow

The wild woman had one last duty to perform before putting the past behind her. Leading the boy with her through the smoking streets and holding the bones out before her, she sang the piper's melancholy and evocative tune to new words. The bones led them down dark alleyways to a basement store. The wild woman hammered a pattern of knocks on the door, which quickly opened. The few in the room raised astonished faces at the sight of her. Yet she had known the code.

Those who were left of the protesters were sitting dispirited round a table, discussing the future. They were bruised, and bandages covered new wounds. At least two of their number were dead, possibly more. Many had simply disappeared, perhaps from fear of further reprisals by the authorities, perhaps from more sinister motives. The group had never had terrorist leanings — they were peace people, gentle anachronisms — but it was almost certain that they had been infiltrated by Black Death.

Almost afraid to look each other in the eye, they were on the point of disbanding, giving up.

The wild woman showed them the picture of the dead protester who looked like Jesus. She told them in her deep and soft voice how he had been killed. She gave them a message they took for his. A message that, banal as it was, instantly began to revive and reunite them.

"Death," she said, "is necessary for life. The seed dies that the tree may grow. There is no ending without beginning."

To the square

Heavy-lidded eyes gazed through dark glass at the blazing city. The chauffeur drove carefully through smoke-filled streets. Behind them, buildings melted to the ground. The singer looked at the white bulk next to her, but his reflecting glasses merely stared ahead.

They drove towards the city square.

Joachim opened his eyes as Mary the Mother burst in on him again. Had she avenged so soon? Had she pitied him at last? She had changed her white robe for one of sunburst yellow, her black hair was tied back.

"Brother Joachim!" she exclaimed in a deeper voice. "Is it you?"

Hurriedly but tenderly for his suffering flesh, she undid his tight bonds. She massaged his hands and feet, easing the painful tingling. She fetched water and gave him drops to drink so that the cup might not touch his ravaged mouth.

"You must go," she said to him. "I can't take you, but I'll show you the way."

Brother Joachim stood up but immediately collapsed again. Supporting him, Mary the Mother walked him round the room until his legs were able again to take his weight.

"Where are your clothes?" she asked.

He shook his head. He had no idea.

"Then wear this," Mary the Mother lifted the sunburst yellow caftan off herself. Underneath was the tight leather costume of the lead singer of The Martyrdom of St Sebastian, tight strips of leather on a man's body. Not Mary, then, after all.

The lead singer helped Joachim into the yellow robe.

"You taught me at school, you know," he said. "All the rivers of the world. I remember them all: those wonderful names. Limpopo, Irrewaddy, Orinoco, Bramhaputra, Dnieper, Hang-chou-fe... Huarco, source of the Amazon."

Joachim looked at him. The face stood out no more than the other from the endless sea of boy's faces, white blanks that had stared up at him. Perhaps that, after all, had been his fundamental mistake.

The lead singer draped Mary the Mother's soft blue cloth around Joachim's head, hiding his mouth. Then lead him by the arm to the door.

"Go. Walk through, turning left when you can. Then you will reach a side door. It is open now, but it will soon be closed. Don't stop, don't delay, or it will be too late."

The lead singer gripped his arm.

"I don't believe what you believe. I don't believe what I think you believe. But respect my lack of belief."

Joachim nodded, not knowing what the man meant. He recognised no boy he had ever taught. He hardly recognised in this solemn figure the cavorting rock megastar he had seen earlier at the concert. The lead singer pushed him out.

"Hurry," he said.

Joachim walked through the rooms steadily, looking round. His light steps hardly disturbed the new silence. People were gazing vacantly into space or at their reflections in long wall mirrors. If they moved, it was slowly. No one paid him any attention. He turned left and found the side door. It was open.

But the boy, the golden boy! He had to take him away. He had at least to try and save him.

Joachim turned back from the door and searched through the rooms of a black-carpeted corridor. He opened cubicle doors and found copulating couples frozen into immobility, caught in a drugged sleep in the midst of congress. Their blue-white faces were fixed in expressions of hate or horror, lust or satisfaction, according to the moment when the powerful drug had overcome them. A man still had his hands round the neck of a woman with his penis in her mouth, his murderous intent clearly expressed on his frozen face, though his hands had lost their force. Her terrified eyes stared up at him, though now sightless. In another room, a daisy chain of six women lay abandoned, head to tail. In yet another, a man and woman held electric prods that sizzled and burned each other's flesh as they slept unaware. Where there were children, Joachim paused to untie their bonds and chafe their blue feet and hands, but he was afraid to wait too long, too late.

He stood in the black-carpeted, body-strewn corridor listening. There was a heavy stillness hardly broken by the breathing of the sleepers. Then at last, away in the distance, he caught the sound of sobbing. He followed the sound into the large hall where he had been at first, clambering over bodies that twitched and shook; past thin women who turned their heads slowly and looked past him, drawing deep on black cigarettes; past the white and sweating Buddha figure of the Empress, sucking his yellow poison; past children clumsily sticking needles into each other, falling back, thumbs in mouths, into each others arms. In a bright corner, the filthy gypsy held the lightly snoring Lucifer in his arms. Or was it snores or was it gurgles, a last rattling in the throat? The filthy gypsy stared fixedly ahead, holding his broken Puck. His empty eyes did not see his latest victim. Beside them, sobbing, curled an unspeakable creature, a beast, a throw-back, filthy and stinking, smeared with excrement, the once golden boy.

Joachim scooped him up, wrapping him in Mary the Mother's soft blue cloth. The boy pressed his face to Joachim's chest and sobbed.

Stepping over and on twitching and shaking bodies, past the Empress, slumped at last in oblivion; past his Negro boy, sipping dregs of yellow poison and grinning wildly, back along the black corridor, past smoking doorways where the silence was at last broken by screams, Joachim strode to the side door. It was locked. He turned back to the room and saw how it was filling with thick green smoke, how the walls melted as green flames flickered. He saw, leaping in the flames, the glittering figure of the lead singer, a flaring torch in his hand, touching it to drapes and cloths, singing to himself as he whirled frenziedly around: *Tonite!!! Tonite!!! The fires are already burning. The bombs are in position. The hairline cracks will widen into jagged chasms. Tonite!!! Tonite!!! The blood is already flowing. It will flow in rivers. Tonite!!! Tonite!!! I have my gun, baby. My gun is cocked, baby. Put my gun in your cunt, baby. I'll blow your mind.*

He asked for it

The Commissioner of Police had pulled all the food out of his pockets and heaped it on his desk. It looked like the contents of a trash can, dead birds, green slime, unspeakable molluscs, truffles like turds. He picked moodily at bits of the food, staring at the seven canvasses propped against the wall. They almost caused him to lose his appetite.

In one, a pig-faced pig in the Commissioner's uniform was kicking the body of a man, whose face, the face of Jesus, gazed out uncompromisingly at the viewer. In another, the pig-faced pig gnawed evidently human bones with grisly appetite. In another, the pig-faced pig held a white-faced doll on his lap, sticking his fat finger up her all too lifelike vagina. In another, the pig-faced pig almost grunted out of the canvas as he trotted on all fours to the rubbish bin and stuck his snout in it, rooting for goodies. In another, the pig-faced pig struck a noble pose, one hand on breast, the other held aloft, a row of medals pinned to his chest, the noble effect ruined, however, by his piggy face and his obscene nakedness, rolls of pink flesh hanging down over a tiny, vestigial penis. In another, the pig-faced pig, crazed with hunger, ripped open his own body and ate his own guts. In the last picture, a she-wolf with the face of the commissioner's predatory wife, simpered grimly as bloody entrails hung from her mouth and her yellow eyes glinted.

The Commissioner was sweating, cold grey drops. He grabbed a tablecloth and wiped his face. Bones fell to the floor with a clatter. Bones? Thoughtfully, trying not to think, the Commissioner picked one up. Then thoughtfully, still not thinking, he started slowly, slowly to gnaw it.

The wildest yet

Back at the party, the little bride of the ambitious young businessman at last managed to break out of the circle of pawing admirers. The body of the judge had been found in the pantry in suspicious circumstances, and everyone wanted to go and take a look.

The masked and helmeted cop warned no one to leave the premises — not that anyone had any intention of so doing. Such excitement! Such potential scandal! Meanwhile, neither the host nor the hostess was anywhere to be found.

The little bride climbed the stairs, followed some way behind by the full-breasted maid, who was looking for her mistress, no doubt to break the tragic news. The little bride walked along the corridor to the Commissioner's wife's bedroom. She paused for a moment, then knocked.

"Who is it?" called the Commissioner's wife.

The businessman's little bride told her.

"Come in darling."

The businessman's little bride obediently opened the door and entered. The Commissioner's wife was gratified to see the baby blues almost pop right out of their sockets once more.

What the little bride saw was this: spread-eagled on the black satin sheets of the bed, hands and feet chained to the bedposts, was the ambitious young businessman. He was almost naked. Naked but for his socks, which was how the little bride knew him, in fact — those dreadful puce-coloured socks he always favoured. His face, however, could not be seen, because, naked, too, the Commissioner's predatory wife was sitting on it.

"Come and join us, darling, I was so hoping you would."

She lifted herself from the businessman's face. "Look who's here, darling," she chuckled. "Now we can really have some fun."

Suddenly there was a peal of laughter from behind the businessman's little wife. The full-breasted maid was laughing delightedly. She gripped the businessman's little bride in a paroxysm of mirth.

"How ridiculous!" she exclaimed. "Have you ever seen anything so funny!"

Suddenly, the businessman's little bride saw how ludicrous it was, too. The pale and rather hairy legs of her ambitious young husband stuck out at angles across the bed like sticks. His penis stood almost erect — it had just started to droop — looking more than ever like the neck of a plucked turkey. His chained arms stuck up awkwardly as if he were making a signal of some sort. Semaphore, perhaps. He stared at his bride in foolish amazement. The Commissioner's wife's make-up was smeared over her face, great black streaks descending from her eyes, a magenta gash across her mouth. What she meant as an enticing smile came out as a grotesque leer. Her cropped purple hair stood on end. Her gnarled breasts hung down almost to her hard ball of a belly. Her buttocks had withered into flaps. As a figure of erotic delight, she was a complete failure.

The businessman's little bride could not after all join in the maid's laughter. She started to weep in pity and sorrow. The face of the full-breasted maid hardened.

"Enough," she said. "The judge is dead."

"What!" screeched the Commissioner's wife, leaping up.

"He died in the pantry," the full-breasted maid explained.

The Commissioner's wife rapidly drew on her dress.

"In the pantry?" She understood nothing. A heart-attack probably. But in the pantry! Was he groping the maids again? The footmen again? What a scandal!

Not pausing to clean up her face, not pausing to release the ambitious young businessman from his bonds, the Commissioner's wife raced along the corridor, down the elegant staircase and into the kitchen where all the guests were peering into the pantry at the prone body of the late judge.

Meanwhile, the full-breasted maid smiled cruelly at the businessman's little bride.

"They made a fool of you, didn't they."

The businessman's little wife sobbed.

"Don't worry, honey. Tonight everyone gets it."

The full-breasted maid crossed over to where the ambitious young businessman lay. She lifted her skirt and pulled out an automatic. Then she shot him through the head.

The horrified little bride (just becoming widow) stared at the last shudderings of her husband for a moment, at the hole in the side of his head, at the smoking blood on the black satin pillow, at the fountain of sperm from the suddenly vertical penis, at the twitching of his feet in those horrible puce socks, until he was quite still. Then she ran off down the corridor and up the stairs to the top of the building, opening a door at random and falling inside.

Downstairs, the shot had been heard by the guests and the Commissioner's wife.

"She killed him!" she exclaimed, thinking the little doll had more in her than you would have imagined by looking at her.

She made as if to run upstairs again, but the handpicked valet restrained her.

"I'll go," he said.

The cop they called Mirandolo ushered all the fascinated guests into the ballroom, with its glittering chandeliers, its gold framed mirrors. Then he stood, arms folded, watching them, the cream of society, the icing on the social cake, the tops dogs, captains of industry, personalities, powers in the land, twittering, excited, not really anxious. Not yet.

"Have you sent for my husband, for reinforcements?" the Commissioner's wife enquired of him

"Everything necessary is being done," the cop said.

Near him now, the Commissioner's wife could smell his pungency. It excited her. A man of real power. A man with a gun.

She licked her lips and gazed at him. It was impossible to read his expression through his mask. She couldn't even tell if he was looking at her.

"You could do it," she whispered. "You could do what no one else can do. You could make me come."

The full-breasted maid entered the room. In the bright light of the chandeliers the blood on her dress could clearly be seen, black gobs of judicial blood.

"Take this one out," the cop they called Mirandolo said. "She deserves special treatment."

The full-breasted maid gripped the astonished Commissioner's wife tightly by the arm and took her to the kitchen, where she locked her in the pantry with the dead judge. Not before they had passed, in the hallway, the handpicked valet with the machine-gun he had collected from his room. The full-breasted maid looked at the valet and asked, "OK?"

The valet nodded, not telling what he had found in his bedroom.

The Commissioner's wife looked at him in horror and with sudden realisation.

"You!" she exclaimed. "You!"

She had picked him herself. For the second time that endless night she had cause to doubt her own judgement.

As the full-breasted maid dragged the Commissioner's wife off to her rendezvous in the pantry, the valet entered the huge and glittering ballroom. The cream of society turned to look at him as he entered, and a gasp shivered through them as they saw what he was holding. The cop they called Mirandolo took the machine gun out of the valet's hands and motioned the cream of society up against the large mirrors. The valet ordered the band to start playing some loud music.

"Plenty of drums and cymbals."

The band started to play the Radetsky March.

Outside in the grounds, the shivering police - from being stiflingly hot it had suddenly become very cold - gazed at the bright windows and thought what a good time some lucky people were having.

"Take your clothes off," the cop they called Mirandolo ordered the cream of society. When they hesitated, he jerked the gun. Off came the expensive suits and shirts, the designer dresses, the soft and silky underwear. Off came the jewellery.

"Well, well," commented the cop they called Mirandolo. "Underneath, you're just like everyone else."

People had taken off their clothes at parties given by the Commissioner's wife before, but this was different. Suddenly sober, they peeped timidly at each other's lumps and uncorseted bulges, only too aware of their own. They looked at the scars on each other's bodies where solid flesh had been surgically removed or implanted, where buttocks had been tightened.

"Dance," the cop they called Mirandolo ordered the cream of society. "Take your partners, ladies and gents please, and DANCE."

And as the cream of society tried to dance to the Radetsky March, as they asked each other if this was yet another of the Commissioner's wife's warped jokes, the cop they called Mirandolo roared out their death sentence and opened fire.

The mirrors cracked, the chandeliers shattered, the bodies toppled into piles, and outside in the freezing night, the cops were thinking that of all wild parties ever held in that house, this one had to be the wildest yet.

They had no right

Upstairs in the valet's room, the room she had stumbled into by chance, the doll-faced young widow was trying to revive the comatose maid. She had released her bonds, slapped her face, breathed into her mouth as she had been taught.

The valet, fetching the machine gun, had paused to show her where the coffee was, how she could use the electric kettle to make some. He was enraged. The full-breasted woman, the man disguised as the cop, they had no right. The cause had not demanded this.

He had paused to look into the unconscious face of the maid, her hair still powdered with golden pollen. He bent his face down to hers, and heard her shallow breath. He inhaled her scent of summer. He pressed his lips to her cold damp forehead. They had no right.

He had told the doll-faced widow she could try to revive the maid. He had told her how she could escape.

Forcing the coffee into the maid's mouth until she choked and vomited. Forcing more coffee into her, dragging her round the room, round the room. The widow heard the explosion of machine-gun fire from the ballroom below, and knew that time was short. Desperately, she dragged the maid over to the window and opened it. Looking out, she saw the spindly fire escape extend down the outside wall of the mansion to the garden far below. She dragged the maid out on to the fire escape. The cold air made her gasp. She propped the maid against the wrought iron, and dashed back into the room for a blanket, which she placed round the maid's trembling shoulders. But the cold air had caused the maid to gasp, too, and now she was swallowing air like wine and laughing as if she were drunk. Slowly, slowly the widow supported her down the fire escape, step by step, rung by rung, always aware of the plunge to the hard as iron garden below if her foot should slip. Down and down and down.

The source

Smoke in his face, smoke that took his breath away, that was taking his life away. Flames catching at his feet, at the sunburst yellow robe. Joachim covered the golden boy's body with his own, huddled against the locked door.

Joachim closed his stinging eyes. The Amazon beckoned, the wide waters of the Amazon. Ucayali, its prime tributary, the Tambo, the Ene, the Apurimac, the Santiago, the Toro. Up up in the Arequiqpa Andes. The source. Huarco, Huarco, Huarco.

Lamb of God

She had crawled up through the split open doors and now crouched at the base of a pillar. Closing her eyes, she found herself at last in the rose garden. She lay down upon the soft grass and rose petals covered her skin. She could smell their intense sweetness. The scent filling her head. A soft and warm breeze insinuated into her hair, lifting it gently. Angels were singing.

She opened her eyes and saw a procession of white-clad nuns, each holding a perfumed candle, walk chanting down the aisles of the cathedral. Smoke swirled above her, veiling the great vault, smoke from the hundreds of perfumed candles. A priest stood at the altar dressed in a heavy robe of embroidered gold thread. He swung a censer, muttering incantations as he did so, perfumed smoke rising. No rose had ever smelt like this. Her heavy eyes closed again. She was no longer in the garden. She was being carried as though she weighed nothing. Her body seemed to grow lighter, she was almost floating. She would have floated away were it not for the firm grasp of the person carrying her. Someone she knew, someone she had once loved and now feared. Up up the stairs on to a landing. She opened her heavy eyes and saw the two of them reflected in a mirror on the landing. Quickly she closed her eyes tight again. She would have liked to float away but the arms held her tight. They placed her on the bed, holding her down (she was struggling now). She felt the now familiar heaviness and pain and shame. She had shut her eyes not to see. She tried to sleep not to feel. Then she awoke and found the woman she called mother beating her with a strap, beating her down down the stairs again (the two of them reflected in the mirror's eye), down and out of the bright and shining house into the conservatory. Locked in the conservatory. Growing huge in the conservatory like a forced fruit, ripening. Banging on the glass, gasping in the heat. Drugged by the foetid smell. Falling... falling. And all the time growing. And then...

She opened her eyes wide. There on the great wooden crucifix over the altar. There. It wasn't true. It couldn't be true.

She got up shakily. She pushed her way up to the altar, past the procession of white and chanting nuns. She stared over the head of the priest at the wooden crucifix, through the swirls of perfumed smoke in the dim candlelight. She pointed a trembling finger at the crucifix.

"At last!" she cried in ecstasy. "I've found you. At last."

Her shout caused several nuns to look at her. Even the priest turned.

"Why are you there?" she called. "What have they done to you?" She looked round wildly. "Why have they done this thing?"

A nun stepped forward.

"It's our Lord Jesus Christ," she said softly to the woman. "They have crucified him."

"Not Jesus," the woman screamed, gripping the nun's shoulder. "My daughter. They are crucifying my daughter."

The nuns looked at the priest in horror. Whispers of "Blasphemy... blasphemy..." ran down the aisles.

The priest stepped forward, glorious in gold, God's representative.

"What are you saying, woman?" he asked, not yet unkindly.

At the sound of his kind voice, the woman looked up.

"There, on the cross... see her... my daughter."

"On the cross?" the priest asked. "No, my dear, you are deluded. It is our blessed Lord Jesus Christ who is on the cross, who died to save our souls. Who died that we might live."

"Blessed be his holy name for ever," chanted the nuns.

"Amen," answered the priest.

"Can't you see her?" the woman persisted. "You must be able to see her."

"My good woman," the priest said rattily, "what you see is the Son of God. God had no daughter."

"The Son of God," chanted the nuns.

"The Son of God with breasts. The Son of God with a...." (what was the word she had heard so recently?) "...with a cunt?"

The nuns gasped in outrage.

"Cast her out, father. This woman is surely the devil."

They all blessed themselves repeatedly and repeated, "Devil. Devil."

"I'm no devil," the woman said. "I'm a mother."

"Ha!" laughed a nun harshly, the same whose shoulder the woman had gripped so tightly. "A mother, is it? Look at yourself. Anyone can see what you are! You filthy harlot."

Another nun pointed to a painting of the Blessed Virgin Mary, white and blue-robed, blue-eyed and coral-lipped, pallid skinned, her face turned heavenwards — the portrait of the missing statue. "That's what a mother looks like. Do you look like that? Do you? Do you?"

A third nun stepped forward, "You should be ashamed to enter here and defile the House of God."

"Get out!" the nuns shouted, clawing at her. "Get out!"

"Father!" the woman cried to the priest, stretching out her hands as the nuns beat her down the aisle. The priest turned away. Her father turned away, as her mother beat her out of the house.

"Get out, you filthy slut!"

"You never bore a child."

"You are as barren as we are."

They whipped at her, tore at her, clawed her.

"Devil! Whore! Bitch! Cunt!"

The ice-blue light on the steps of the floodlit cathedral illuminated the racked body of the woman where she lay. The nuns retreated inside, calm restored, resuming their procession and their chant.

Agnus Dei
qui tollis peccata mundi:
miserer nobis.
Agnus Dei,
qui tollis peccata mundi:
dona nobis pacem.

All my daughters

The woman lay still on the ground outside the cathedral. Mary the Mother, blazing white, stood at her feet, gazing down.

"It's not true," the woman whispered to her. "This is my daughter. They are all my daughters. They are crucifying all my daughters. They say I never bore a child. That's not true. How could they know? How could they say that? I delivered my daughter myself. I saw her. Five months in the womb and perfectly formed. You wouldn't believe that possible, would you? Only five months and perfect in every way. And beautiful. I could hold her in my one hand, so tiny she was. Like a …. like a doll, and so still and cold. Like a doll. Then they came and took her away from me. They took my darling away from me."

Blowing your mind

"You know," the terrorist dressed as the cop they called Mirandolo was saying to the valet, "this lady is a big fan of The Martyrdom of St Sebastian. Isn't that a howl."

They had left the ballroom where the band played on, guarded by the full-breasted woman who now toted the machine-gun, tapping her foot to the rhythm of the dance. They had gone to the kitchen and opened the door to the pantry, where they had found the Commissioner's crazy old wife trying to copulate with the dead judge. She laughed when they opened the door.

"They old bugger can't get it up," she giggled. "I always suspected it."

"Tonite!!!" crooned the terrorist dressed as Mirandolo, while the Commissioner's wife caressed him. "The blood is already flowing. It will flow in rivers. Tonite!!!"

"All your guests are dead, you know," the valet said to the Commissioner's wife as she ran her claw inside the so-called cop's shirt and sniffed the overpowering pungency of the late Mirandolo.

"She doesn't care," the terrorist told him, roughly pushing the Commissioner's wife back on the floor and ripping her skirt. The Commissioner's wife closed her eyes and lifted her legs.

"Tonite!!!" whispered the terrorist disguised as the cop. "Tonite!!!"

He took out his gun.

"I have my gun, baby," he crooned. "My gun is cocked, baby. Put my gun in your cunt, baby…" the Commissioner's wife, without opening her eyes, took the gun barrel and stuck it between her legs. The fake cop viciously pushed it up harder. The Commissioner's wife started to rock violently. She screamed and ululated. The valet looked away from them both in disgust. Each was as bad as the other.

The fake cop crooned on, "Put my gun in your cunt, baby. I'll blow your mind."

"Yes," screamed the Commissioner's wife. "Yes, yes, oh yes."

The terrorist dressed as Mirandolo pulled the trigger. The Commissioner's wife's yellow eyes popped out of their sockets and rolled away across the floor. Her whole body rose up, then flopped back.

The terrorist dressed as Mirandolo had no time to enjoy his kill. The handpicked valet stuck a carving knife into his back, whispering, "That's for the innocent victims."

But the screams of pleasure of the Commissioner's wife had at last alerted the cops freezing in the garden. They burst through the door in time to see the valet stabbing a cop. They all shot him at once, his body dancing in the air.

The full-breasted maid, hearing them coming, detonated the bomb under her dress that was to blow up the whole house, and for a moment the sky over the city was again illuminated by a light that was as bright as the sun.

Rose red

Long long ago, in a time before time, a young girl had broken out of a glass conservatory that had been her prison, and had started to crawl — for she was very weak — up an endless flight of stairs in a bright house, where light fell in white bands across the carpet of the stairs, now spotted with the young girl's blood. And she had crawled step by step up the stairs to a terrible room — her own room, her darling's room. She had climbed, smashing her ribs on each step, despite the soft carpeting, and had crawled towards the door of her room. She had pushed the door open with her shaking hand and saw... She had screamed at the sight of a gypsy woman in a flame-coloured skirt holding a baby that was no bigger than a doll, winding the baby tightly in rags. The gypsy woman had turned and laughed at the girl, flashing white and gold teeth. She had called out something in a Romany language the girl could not understand. The girl had screamed, for she had recognised the baby. The gypsy woman had thrown the bundle at her and had run past her down the stairs, cackling with laughter, and the girl had hugged the baby to her. But when the girl unwrapped the bundle, it was just stinking rags. The baby was gone.

The girl had screamed and torn at her hair. She had hammered on the floor and on the walls in a frenzy of grief and anger, sobbing tears that burned and sizzled. Then she had noticed for the first time two grey old people in the room with her, cowering against the wall, viewing her with terrified eyes. The girl had seized the strap and had driven them down the stairs and out of the house. Then she had run exultantly into the conservatory and broken all the windows. At last, exhausted, she had climbed out into the rose garden and, drinking in the soft and aromatic air, petals floating about her, landing lightly on her, had fallen asleep. When she had awakened, it was night and spiders had already taken over the house. For days, the girl had waited but no one returned. For weeks, for years, she had waited and dust covered the brightness and coated the windows, blotting out the light. Only the spiders moved busily, weaving. And the rose bushes grew up round the house and in through the conservatory, pushing up at the windows of the spidery house, and finally the girl forgot what she was waiting for.

Then one beautiful sunshiny morning, the girl, who had now become a middle-aged woman, woke up at last and left the spidery house to go out into the world.

Pig

A fragment of bone sticking in his throat, the Police Commissioner hopped and danced around his office. He grabbed at the buttons of his uniform, his collar buttons, taut against his flesh, but could not open them. No one could open them but the nimble fingers of his handpicked valet. The Commissioner tore at his neck.

Skipping in to join the dance came his victims, led by the protester who looked like Jesus, smiling but cadaverous as if he had spent three days in the tomb. As the Commissioner snorted and grunted in his efforts to breathe, his victims danced around him merrily. The Commissioner sank to his knees. He felt his body swelling. At last - pop! pop! - his buttons flew off, his clothes fell from him. He coughed, and the fragment of bone dropped from his gullet. Snorting and snuffling, the erstwhile Commissioner trotted round his office on all fours, blundering and banging into furniture, toppling plants, smearing pictures, knocking a framed photograph of a grimly simpering woman to the floor and smashing its glass with his trotters.

At last, one of the cachinating victims took pity on the frenzied beast and opened the office door, whereupon the rest shooed it out on to the staircase. The gigantic pig slipped and slithered down into the city square and off away out into the endless night.

What happened in the square

The girl-child in the red dress walked purposefully, her arm outstretched in front of her.

The officer-in-charge at the police station sent out an all personnel alert for the piper.

The white limousine purred through the streets as the city melted around it.

An exhausted procession of dwarfs and midgets, the strong man carrying the ugly midget on his shoulders, the bearded lady still dragging the little trolley bearing the limbless man, trod steaming alleyways, progressing inexorably onwards.

Down down down from the mountain sped the piper for the second time that night, like a streak of moonlight, down to his beloved who lay covered now in a soft veil of spiders' webs, tiny spiders weaving in and out of her soft red hair, as the house sighed and slept.

As the piper burst for the third time that endless night naked into the city square, the second officer stepped out of the police station, while the white limousine, the procession of midgets and dwarfs, the girl child in the red dress, all converged on the square together. The second officer, not pausing to think, raised his service revolver and shot the piper dead. The ugly midget lifted his face to the dark night and howled, Mishka spread his hands in despair, and the rest of the group fell to the ground sobbing. The door of the limousine opened and the white bandaged singer jumped out and tore across the square to the body of her only beloved. She fell on his body and kissed his silver skin. She covered his silver body with kisses and would have stayed thus forever, kissing the eyes that had never seen her and would now never see her, the mouth that had never spoken to her, never opened in a kiss. The chauffeur got out of the limousine and crossed the square to where she was. He tried to prise her from the body of the piper but she clung on tightly. The chauffeur wound her long black hair round his hand and dragged her from the piper's silver body. At the last minute, she grabbed the tin whistle from the piper's tightening grasp as the chauffeur dragged her away. He tugged and dragged her across the square to the limousine, where Mr El Blanco waited, staring through his reflecting glasses. By the time they reached the limousine, the singer's black hair had turned white. Mr El Blanco looked at her for a minute. He took off his reflecting glasses and put his face down close to her. She looked into his uncovered eyes and shuddered. For the first time, no matter what the gossips said, for the first time ever he kissed her lips, looking deep into her eyes. In a moment, her beautiful body withered, her face grew haggard. She was an old woman and now could remember everything: the two children who had grown up together, offspring of the same parents. The brother who had stared deep into his sister's eyes and made her do unspeakable things. The brother who had taken the sister's children as they sprang from her body. She had spent her whole life in a trance and now had woken to find her life nearly gone and her hands empty.

Mr El Blanco put on his reflecting sunglasses again. He turned away.

The chauffeur jeered at her. "Old hag. He don't want you now. No one don't want you now. Your friend certainly don't want you now. You wanna know who wants you now. The worms, that's who."

The old singer stood up, the bandages falling from her withered body, now covered in a wondrous veil of white hair.

"I still have my voice," she said with dignity and began to sing a low blues song.

The dwarfs and midgets drew round her and began to join in. Rodolpho played his mandolin. Exotic birds circles over their heads.

Suddenly, at a gestures from El Blanco, the chauffeur hit the singer hard across the throat. She fell to the ground.

"Sing now," the chauffeur mocked her. "Sing now, if you can."

The singer staggered to her feet and tried again to sing, but all that came out was a hoarse croak.

The strong man slowly put the ugly midget down on the ground. He slowly advanced on the chauffeur, who tried to back off but was hemmed in on all sides by midgets and dwarfs. The strong man seized hold of the chauffeur and spun him round his head several times before flinging him into the darkest corner of the square, breaking every large bone in his body.

Mr El Blanco gazed imperturbably at the scene. Behind him, from the shadowy nooks, advanced his ever-present minions. They faced the midgets and dwarfs, grinning with anticipation. Suddenly the girl child in the red dress stepped forwards. She had been staring fixedly at El Blanco. Now she began to walk towards him, her hand stretched out.

"Bonbons," she chanted in a high, shrill voice. "Bonbons."

El Blanco smiled paternally. He recognised all his children, he recognised this girl child. A minion passed him a bag of bonbons and he beckoned the girl child to come to him. She walked through the crowd of midgets and dwarfs and walked through the shadowy minions, her hand outstretched. With the tip of her finger she touched Mr El Blanco, still smiling down at her. And as she touched him, he exploded, his huge body flying in all directions, the skin of his face, still wearing reflecting sunglasses, still wearing his homburg, flying straight up from his skull and fixing itself on a street lamp, where it grinned down luminously on the crowd below.

Burn Burn Burn

Someone must have opened the locked door and pulled him out. Pulled out the golden boy, too, clinging to him, skin singed clean again. Joachim held the boy gently and looked at the remains of the building, a heap of charred rubble on the ground. And around them in all directions, the city burned into other heaps of charred rubble. A huge pig rushed past them wildly, crazed by the smoke and heat.

Yet away from the fires, it was no longer hot. Quite the opposite. Large flakes of snow had started to float down out of the sky, settling on pavements and streets, even on charred heaps of buildings.

Joachim lifted the golden boy up in his arms as if he weighed nothing, and started walking out of the city.

Another one

As Mary the Mother re-entered the cathedral, the nuns turned to look at her. Her white dress was stained and scorched, she had lost her blue headcloth (given to Joachim) her hair fell about her shoulders in wild hanks, her face was spattered with blood.

"Another one!" they screeched at the priest. "Another one!"

The priest turned away, glorious in gold, God's representative.

"Get out!" the nuns shouted. "Clear off!"

Mary the Mother looked at them calmly. Then she looked around at the solid pillars of grey stone, the soaring vault that pinned all aspirations down to earth. She took a huge breath and blew. The puzzled saints watched her.

"Help me," she called to them.

St John and St Thomas and St Martin de Porres and St Mary Magdalen and St Elizabeth turned their stiff faces up up to the soaring vault and blew with Mary the Mother, and finally the huge roof lifted off and flew up away and out of sight.

The astonished nuns, the amazed priest, watched it go, unable to move. Unable to move ever again.

Away

A small train of survivors clustered together in a procession walking away from what remained of the city. The singer, an old old woman sitting on the shoulders of the strong man and wearing a large-sized chocolate and banana coloured hounds tooth jacket, led the way playing a haunting tune on the tin whistle while exotic birds fluttered round her shoulders. Joachim followed, gently leading the golden boy, who now smiled up at him. The doll-like little widow and the languid maid with pollen-dusted hair clung together under a blanket, stumbling occasionally on sharp stones. A band of midgets and dwarfs, a limbless man on a trolley, tugged sometimes by a bearded lady, sometime by an older, fatter woman who once had been an alderman's voluptuous wife, a thin girl-child in a red dress, now able to touch and not destroy, an artist-woman of many colours — the paint having stuck permanently to her skin — arm-in-arm with a boy and each of them clutching a bone, a tramp holding a key for which one day he hoped to find a lock, some peaceniks holding on high a banner poster based on the artist who looked like Jesus — but alive again, deathless — all trudged along the snow covered road that led away from the city. While bouncing behind them, grinning from ear to ear, an almost fleshless skull, the dead tourist not wanting to be left behind.

Pretty as a picture

The snow fell on the city, on the open wounds and bandaged them, rose in heaps on burnt-out or bombed buildings, on city square and city waste land, on concert hall and on mansion, on club and on bar. Covered the body of the piper dead in the square, covered the spidery house with its sleeping secrets, fell into the roofless cathedral, freezing the cold-hearted nuns where they stood, delighting the saints, who built snow-angels and played snowballs, sliding down the icy aisles. Covered the old crone clutching to her again the avenged body of her cat Francis, covered the lads in their basement, the fat whore and the philosopher pimp, the old woman in the crooked ginger wig and the old crock with the pendulous wart.

All that moved in the city now was an ugly midget searching, searching for his lost fiancée and howling to the dark, a gigantic pig rooting in rotten rubbish for something, anything, to eat, a woman dragging herself through the snow, emptied now, dragging herself back back to the city square for something that she

remembered. Slowly dragging herself back into the square to where a baby in a pram, abandoned at last by her mother, tick tocked quietly in the doorway of the police station. The woman dragged herself at long last to the pram and peered in. What a beautiful baby! And abandoned now. How could people abandon their babies and in such cold, too. She put a soiled and tattered rag doll in with the baby to keep her company. Then the woman pushed the pram, with difficulty, up the stairs to where she could hear voices.

She bounced the pram backwards up the stairs — gently, not to wake the sleeping infant — to where the two officers were standing in an open doorway. They were gazing

dumbfounded into the Commissioner's devastated office at the porcine portraits of their chief. The woman pushed the pram in behind them.

"Gentlemen," she said so softly that they didn't hear her at first. "Gentlemen, I've found her. I thought you should be the first to know."

The two officers, laughing uncontrollably now at the portraits, particularly at the one that showed the Commissioner to have such a tiny penis, finally turned to look at her, hardly able to recognise in this wild apparition the mother who had been haunting them all endless night long.

"See how pretty she is. Like a picture," she said proudly, stepping back, stepping down, stepping out. As the two men bent thoughtlessly to look, the bomb at last went off, the last bomb in the city.

A trick of the light

Away already far across the plain, the walkers paused at the sound of the explosion and looked back, and saw at first only a black column of smoke against the whitening sky. Then they saw the tiny figure of the woman staggering towards them, apparently, though it was surely a trick of this new light, supported by another woman, all in white.

"Mary the mother!" Joachim thought.

But there was no one else. They could see that, as the woman staggered towards them, smiling. A trick of the light, no more.

While the others waited, the girl-child in the red dress ran back to meet the woman, taking her hand and bringing her forwards to join them. Then, led by the old singer, playing merrily now on the piper's tin whistle, the procession walked on steadily. Trudging away along a snowy road that wound round the mountain and off over the endless plain towards the sea or towards the source, glimpsing behind the heavy clouds from moment to moment a pinker gleam.

While in the square, unseen — there was no one left to see — the face of Mr El Blanco hanging over the street lamp, shook and shuddered with suppressed mirth, until finally he could hold it in no longer, and his loud ringing laughter rolled out over the empty city. Then the mask of skin fell off the lamp on to the ground, where it was later eaten by a snuffling pig.